3 MINUTES
with
Jesus

3 MINUTES *with* Jesus

180 Devotions for Kids

JEAN FISCHER

BARBOUR **kidz**
A Division of Barbour Publishing

© 2023 by Barbour Publishing, Inc.

3 Minutes with Jesus: 180 Devotions for Girls ISBN 978-1-63609-600-1

3 Minutes with Jesus: 180 Devotions for Boys ISBN 978-1-63609-599-8

All rights reserved. No part of this publication may be reproduced or transmitted for commercial purposes, except for brief quotations in printed reviews, without written permission of the publisher. Reproduced text may not be used on the World Wide Web.

Churches and other noncommercial interests may reproduce portions of this book without the express written permission of Barbour Publishing, provided that the text does not exceed 500 words or 5 percent of the entire book, whichever is less, and that the text is not material quoted from another publisher. When reproducing text from this book, include the following credit line: "From *3 Minutes with Jesus: 180 Devotions for Kids*, published by Barbour Publishing, Inc. Used by permission."

Unless otherwise indicated, all Scripture quotations are taken from the New Life Version copyright © 1969 and 2003 by Barbour Publishing, Inc., Uhrichsville, Ohio 44683. All rights reserved.

Scripture quotations marked cev are from the Contemporary English Version, Copyright © 1995 by American Bible Society. Used by permission.

Scripture quotations marked skjv are taken from the Simplified KJV, copyright © 2022 by Barbour Publishing, Inc., Uhrichsville, Ohio 44683. All rights reserved.

Published by Barbour Publishing, Inc., 1810 Barbour Drive, Uhrichsville, Ohio 44683, www.barbourbooks.com

Our mission is to inspire the world with the life-changing message of the Bible.

Printed in China.

001620 0623 HA

INTRODUCTION

How well do you know Jesus? He knows you inside and out. The Bible has a lot to say about Him, but school, friends, sports, and activities could leave you with little time to sit and read, read, read. That's what makes this devotional so perfect for you! These three-minute readings are just right to help you get to know Jesus a little at a time. Here's what each power-packed devotion looks like:

- Minute 1: Read and think about a scripture verse taken from God's Word, the Bible.

- Minute 2: Learn something about Jesus.

- Minute 3: Use the prayer starter to spend time with Him in prayer.

Of course, these devotions aren't supposed to take the place of regular Bible reading. They're just a fun way to help you get in the habit of spending time with Jesus every day. As you read, remember to share what you learn with your family and friends. Then they will know Jesus too.

Jesus is ready to tell you His story. So what are you waiting for? Let's get started!

But these are written so you may believe that Jesus is the Christ, the Son of God.

JOHN 20:31

JESUS, SON OF GOD

*"For God so loved the world that
He gave His only begotten Son, that
whoever believes in Him should not
perish but have everlasting life."*

JOHN 3:16 SKJV

Jesus' story begins with a problem: sin—people doing and saying things that God says are wrong. God wants everyone to live with Him in heaven after they die, and He knew they couldn't get there with all that sin in their lives. There's no place for sin in heaven. It can't exist there. God understood that people couldn't get rid of sin on their own. So, because He loves us, God sent His only Son, Jesus, to earth with a plan to make it possible for everyone to get to heaven. It was an amazing plan that would take many years. How did Jesus get to earth? God sent Him here as a baby in a human body.

Dear Jesus, I want to learn more about You. . .

MARY, THE CHOSEN ONE

*"Therefore the Lord Himself shall give you a
sign. Behold, a virgin shall conceive and bear
a son and shall call His name Immanuel."*
ISAIAH 7:14 SKJV

God chose a woman named Mary to be baby Jesus' mother.
He sent an angel to Mary, and when she saw him, she was
afraid. "Don't be afraid!" the angel, Gabriel, said. "God
says, 'You are to become a mother and have a Son. You are
to give Him the name Jesus'" (Luke 1:31). *But how will this
happen?* Mary thought. (She was only engaged to her friend
Joseph.) *I'm not married yet. I can't have a baby.* "The Holy
Spirit will come on you," Gabriel answered. "The holy Child
you give birth to will be called the Son of God" (Luke 1:35).
Mary was willing to do whatever God wanted, so she told
Gabriel, "Let it happen to me as you have said" (Luke 1:38).

**Dear Jesus, Your mother trusted God.
Help me trust Him too. . .**

BETHLEHEM

"[Bethlehem,] from you One will come who will rule for Me in Israel. His coming was planned long ago, from the beginning."

MICAH 5:2

The Roman emperor Caesar Augustus ordered that everyone in his nation should be counted. They needed to go to their hometowns, where a count would take place. Joseph was from Bethlehem. So, he and Mary traveled there. The trip was long, and it took several days. There were no cars then. Mary and Joseph walked. We don't know for sure, but Mary may have ridden part of the way on a donkey. She was pregnant with Jesus, and walking would have been very difficult on the rough, unpaved trails. There were hills to cross on the way. Surely, when they arrived in Bethlehem, Mary was very tired.

Dear Jesus, today's Bible verse says God planned from the beginning for You to be born in Bethlehem. There isn't anything God doesn't know. He has all things planned from beginning to end. . .

JESUS IS BORN

*And so it was, that while they were
there. . .she brought forth her firstborn son,
and wrapped Him in swaddling cloths,
and laid Him in a manger, because there
was no room for them in the inn.*
LUKE 2:6–7 SKJV

Bethlehem was a busy place filled with visitors who had
arrived to be counted. When Joseph and Mary got there,
all the rooms where they might have stayed were already
taken. There was no place for them. So, they went to where
the animals were kept. Some people think it was a stable;
others say a cave. The Bible doesn't tell us. But in that place
Mary gave birth to baby Jesus. She wrapped Him in cloth
to keep Him warm, and she laid Him in a manger—a long,
straw-filled feeding box for animals.

---

*Dear Jesus, You were a special baby, God's Son, but there
was nothing fancy about the place You were born. . .*

SHEPHERDS AND ANGELS

*"For to you is born this day in the city of
David a Savior, who is Christ the Lord."*
LUKE 2:11 SKJV

It was nighttime. Shepherds were nearby in the fields watching over their sheep when an angel appeared to them in a bright, heavenly light. The light was so bright it frightened the shepherds. The angel said to them, "Do not be afraid. See! I bring you good news of great joy. . . . [The] One Who saves from the punishment of sin has been born. . . . He is Christ the Lord" (Luke 2:10–11). Then the angel told them where to find baby Jesus. Many other angels joined in, all giving thanks to God and saying, "Glory to God in the highest, and on earth peace, goodwill toward men" (Luke 2:14 SKJV).

---

*Dear Jesus, God's plan for You was just beginning. No
one knew yet the amazing things You would do. . .*

JESUS' MANY NAMES

For to us a Child will be born. To us a Son will be given. And the rule of the nations will be on His shoulders. His name will be called Wonderful, Teacher, Powerful God, Father Who Lives Forever, Prince of Peace.

ISAIAH 9:6

Long before Jesus was born, prophets—men and women who spoke for God—delivered God's message that the "Messiah," the One who would save them from sin, was coming. One of the prophets, Isaiah, listed some other names Jesus would be called: Wonderful, Teacher, Powerful God, Father Who Lives Forever, Prince of Peace. And later, other names were added: Savior, Christ, Lord. Someday, everyone would know that Jesus wasn't just God's Son. He was a part of God with all of God's power, and He along with God would rule heaven and earth, forever.

---

*Dear Jesus, I know another name for You:
Friend. You are my best friend. . .*

SIMEON

"He will be a light to shine on the people who are not Jews. He will be the shining-greatness of Your people the Jews."
LUKE 2:32

The shepherds visited baby Jesus. They told Mary what the angel had said, and Mary thought much about the angel's words. There were other visitors too who had messages from God. One was an old man named Simeon. He held baby Jesus and said, "My eyes have seen the One Who will save men from the punishment of their sins" (Luke 2:30). But then Simeon said something else to Mary, something no mother wanted to hear, a hint about what would happen to Jesus in the future, another bit of God's plan. "He will be spoken against," Simeon said. "A sword [of sadness] will cut through your soul" (Luke 2:34–35). No one knew yet exactly what it meant. But Mary certainly thought about those words too.

Dear Jesus, Mary was strong and still trusted God after hearing those words. I want that kind of strength...

ANNA

*At that time she came and gave thanks to God.
She told the people in Jerusalem about Jesus.*
LUKE 2:38

Mary and Joseph took Jesus to the temple (the temple was a lot like a church), and Anna was there praying. The Bible tells us Anna was very old and a widow—her husband had died. She was at the temple day and night praying to God. Sometimes, she even went without food so she could think only on Him and pray better. Anna was a prophet who spoke God's words, and as soon as she saw baby Jesus, she knew He was the one who would save everyone from sin. Anna gave thanks to God, and then she shared the good news with others. The news about Jesus began to spread. The Messiah, the Promised One, had arrived.

---

*Dear Jesus, help me be more like Anna and
focus only on You when I pray. . .*

WISE MEN FROM THE EAST

"Where is He who is born King of the Jews? For we have seen His star in the East and have come to worship Him."

MATTHEW 2:2 SKJV

Wise men from the East remembered what ancient prophets said about God sending the Messiah. When a bright star appeared in the sky, they believed it was a sign. They followed the star to Jerusalem, and there they asked directions from Herod, the king. When Herod heard that Jesus had come, he worried this King of the Jews would take over his kingdom. Herod told the men, "When you have found Him, bring me word again, that I may come and worship Him also" (Matthew 2:8 SKJV). But Herod did not plan to worship Jesus. Instead, he planned to kill Him. The wise men found Jesus in Bethlehem. They bowed and worshipped Him and gave Him gifts: gold and two kinds of incense—frankincense and myrrh.

Dear Jesus, please teach me how to worship You. . .

WORSHIP THE KING

"It is written, 'You shall worship the Lord your God, and you shall serve Him only.'"
LUKE 4:8 SKJV

The wise men understood why they should worship Jesus. Although He looked every bit like a human baby and had flesh and bones like every other human, Jesus' soul—the part that makes us who we are inside our hearts—was different. In His soul Jesus wasn't human at all. He was God! It was as if God had sent a part of Himself into the world inside a human body. We worship Jesus today because we know what the wise men knew: Jesus is the King of all kings, God, our Savior, the One who came to save us from sin. We worship Him by believing in who He is, doing our best to please Him, and making Him more important than anything else in our lives.

Dear Jesus, remind me to always put You first and to behave in ways that please You...

"FLEE TO EGYPT!"

*"When Israel was a child, I loved him
and called My son out of Egypt."*

HOSEA 11:1 SKJV

Did the wise men return to Jerusalem to King Herod and tell him where baby Jesus was? No, they did not! In a dream, God warned them to go home another way. And when Herod found out, he was angry. Not knowing which baby was Jesus, he ordered that all baby boys who were two years old or younger and lived in or near Bethlehem should be killed. An angel came to Joseph in a dream. "Arise," the angel said, "and take the young Child and His mother, and flee into Egypt, and stay there until I bring you word" (Matthew 2:13 SKJV). So, in the middle of the night, Mary and Joseph hurried off with Jesus to Egypt. They stayed there safely until the angel returned and told them that King Herod had died.

---

*Dear Jesus, God's angels were always watching
over You. I believe they watch over me too...*

A NEW HOME

And he came and dwelled in a city
called Nazareth, that it might be fulfilled
what was spoken by the prophets:
"He shall be called a Nazarene."
MATTHEW 2:23 SKJV

How long did Jesus and His parents stay in Egypt? The Bible doesn't tell us. But when they left for a new place, Jesus wasn't a tiny baby anymore. After King Herod died, God came to Joseph in a dream and told him not to go back to the area where Jesus was born. Herod's son had become king and ruled the land there. They should go instead to an area known as Galilee. So, the family packed up and left. Soon they settled into a new home in a city called Nazareth. That's where Jesus grew up. We don't know much about His childhood, but in many ways, Jesus was a kid just like you.

Dear Jesus, You were a boy once, so I think
You know what it's like to be a kid. . .

JESUS AT THE TEMPLE

"I came down from heaven. I did not come to do what I wanted to do. I came to do what My Father wanted Me to do. He is the One Who sent Me."

JOHN 6:38

When Jesus was twelve, His family traveled to a festival in Jerusalem. On the way home, while walking in a crowd (imagine your family leaving after watching fireworks or a parade) they realized Jesus wasn't with them. His parents panicked. Where was He? They finally found Him at the temple listening to the teachers talk about God. *"Where were You!"* His mother said. Jesus answered, "Why were you looking for Me? Do you not know that I must be in My Father's house?" (Luke 2:49). Mary remembered that her little boy was the Son of God. He wasn't lost. He was exactly where God wanted Him to be.

Dear Jesus, if I get lost, You will know exactly where I am. You will find me. . .

ELIZABETH AND ZACHARIAS

"He will be the one to go in the spirit and power of Elijah* before Christ comes. He will turn the hearts of the fathers back to their children. He will teach those who do not obey to be right with God. He will get people ready for the Lord."

Luke 1:17

Mary's cousin Elizabeth and Elizabeth's husband, Zacharias, wanted children, but they had none. Now they were too old. But God's angel, Gabriel, came to Zacharias and said, "Elizabeth will give birth to a son. You are to name him John" (Luke 1:13). When Zacharias wasn't sure, Gabriel told him, "God sent me to bring you this good news." Before long, although it had been very unlikely because she was too old, Elizabeth knew she was pregnant. God had great plans for baby John. Gabriel said to Zacharias, "He will get people ready for the Lord" (Luke 1:17).

Dear Jesus, God can do anything. . .

---

* Elijah was an ancient prophet who urged people to turn from sin and follow God.

COUSIN JOHN

The news of what had happened was told
through all the hill country of Judea. And all
who heard those words remembered them
and said, "What is this child going to be?"
For the hand of the Lord was on him.
LUKE 1:65–66

When Gabriel told Mary she would give birth to Jesus, he said something else too. "See, your cousin Elizabeth, as old as she is, is going to give birth to a child. She was not able to have children before, but now she is in her sixth month" (Luke 1:36). So Mary went to see Elizabeth. And when the baby inside Elizabeth heard Mary's voice, he moved with joy. Excited, Elizabeth spoke to Mary: "You are honored among women! Your Child is honored!" (Luke 1:42). "My heart sings with thanks for my Lord," Mary answered (Luke 1:46). Three months later, Jesus' cousin John was born.

Dear Jesus, although You were God, You had a human family with parents, siblings, and cousins—just like me! . . .

GOD'S PLAN FOR JOHN

*"I am the voice of one crying in the desert.
'Make the road straight for the Lord.'"*
JOHN 1:23

Long before John was born, the prophet Isaiah spoke about him. Isaiah said, "[Listen and hear] the voice of him who cries in the wilderness: 'Prepare the way of the LORD'" (Isaiah 40:3 SKJV). When baby John grew up, he lived in the wilderness. He wore clothes made of camel hair, and he ate wild locusts and honey. God's plan for John (who would be called John the Baptist) was to preach and to baptize people in the Jordan River. They confessed their sins, and then John dunked them briefly into the water. It was a symbolic way of making their souls clean before worshipping God. John told the people, "One is coming after me Who is greater than I. . . . I have baptized you with water. But He will baptize you with the Holy Spirit" (Mark 1:7–8). He was speaking about Jesus.

---

*Dear Jesus, I wonder what God has
planned for me when I grow up. . .*

JESUS IS BAPTIZED

*"He who puts his trust in Me and is baptized
will be saved from the punishment of sin.
But he who does not put his trust in Me
is guilty and will be punished forever."*
MARK 16:16

Jesus had grown up too. He was just six months younger
than John. One day, when John was at the river baptizing
people, he saw Jesus there waiting to be baptized. John knew
Jesus was more than just his human cousin—He was God's
Son. John thought, *Who am I to baptize Him? God's Son
doesn't need to be baptized!* He said to Jesus, "But, I should
be baptized by *You*!" Still, Jesus wanted John to baptize
Him. "Let it be done," Jesus said. "We should do what is
right" (Matthew 3:15). So, John agreed and baptized Him.

---

*Dear Jesus, when people are baptized today, it is a
way of remembering You. When we are baptized, our
hearts connect with You in a very special way. . .*

GOD SPEAKS

"The LORD has said to Me, 'You are My Son; this day I have become Your Father.'"

PSALM 2:7 SKJV

Jesus had traveled more than fifty miles from His home in Nazareth, in the country called Galilee, to be baptized by John in the Jordan River. Some important Bible events had occurred at the Jordan River. The Old Testament says that many years earlier God's people, the Israelites, crossed over that river and into the special homeland God had promised them. Maybe that's why God wanted Jesus baptized there. When John baptized Him, Jesus came up out of the water and the sky opened up! The Holy Spirit of God came down and rested on Him like a dove. Then a voice was heard from heaven. It said, "This is My beloved Son, in whom I am well pleased" (Matthew 3:17 SKJV).

Dear Jesus, I feel happy when someone says they are pleased with me. You must have felt happy when Your Father said He was pleased with You...

"THIS IS THE ONE!"

John spoke about [Jesus] and shouted,
"This is the one I told you would come!
He is greater than I am, because he
was alive before I was born."
JOHN 1:15 CEV

After he baptized Jesus, John shouted to the crowd, "This is the One I told you about, the One who would come." The people had heard about God sending a Messiah to save them from sin. Some thought John was the Messiah because he baptized people. But John told them, "No! Jesus is greater than I am because He was alive before I was born." John knew that Jesus had been with God forever. Nothing had ever been created without God and Jesus doing it together. Jesus and God were one. Jesus had all of God's power to do great things, and although He had come to earth in a human body for a while, Jesus was God.

Dear Jesus, now I understand! You were God Himself
coming down to earth to live among the people. . .

THE DEVIL AND SIN

*"The devil has nothing to do with the truth.
There is no truth in him. It is expected of the
devil to lie, for he is a liar and the father of lies."*

JOHN 8:44

Adam and Eve were the first humans on earth. God created them and a beautiful, perfect garden to live in. He gave them just one rule: not to eat fruit from one of the trees, the Tree of Learning of Good and Bad. But the devil, who was disguised as a serpent, used lies to tempt Adam and Eve to disobey. When they did, sin entered the world. Adam and Eve could have obeyed God, but they chose instead to obey the devil. What was once perfect in every way became destroyed by sin. And the devil continued trying to get people to disobey God. That's why God needed to send us Jesus.

---

*Dear Jesus, I'm grateful God sent You to save
us from sin and the devil's evil lies. . .*

THE DEVIL TEMPTS JESUS

Christ was tempted in every way we
are tempted, but He did not sin.
HEBREWS 4:15

After Jesus was baptized, He went alone into the desert for forty days. While Jesus was in the desert, the devil kept trying to trick Him into turning away from God. He tempted Him. That means the devil tested Jesus to see if Jesus would choose his way or God's. For forty days and nights, the devil tried to get Jesus to mess up. But Jesus wouldn't give in. He stood up for what He knew was right and good. Finally, Jesus commanded the devil, "Get away, Satan. It is written, 'You must worship the Lord your God. You must obey Him only'" (Matthew 4:10). Then the devil obeyed Jesus and went away.

Dear Jesus, when I feel tempted to do something I
know is wrong, will You help me not to give in?...

THE LORD'S PRAYER

*"Watch and pray so that you will not be
tempted. Man's spirit is willing, but the
body does not have the power to do it."*
MATTHEW 26:41

Jesus says we need to watch out for the devil trying to tempt us. He gave us a special prayer called "the Lord's Prayer." It's a prayer you should memorize. When you feel the devil tempting you, or anytime you need to feel closer to God, you can say this prayer:

Our Father who is in heaven, hallowed be Your name. Your kingdom come. Your will be done on earth as it is in heaven. Give us this day our daily bread. And forgive us our debts, as we forgive our debtors. And do not lead us into temptation, but deliver us from evil. For Yours is the kingdom and the power and the glory forever. Amen. (Matthew 6:9–13 SKJV)

**Dear Jesus, I will memorize the Lord's Prayer
and keep it inside my heart. . .**

ISAIAH, THE PROPHET

*The people who walk in darkness will see
a great light. The light will shine on those
living in the land of dark shadows.*
ISAIAH 9:2

The prophet Isaiah lived in Jerusalem long before Jesus was born. God often spoke to him, giving him messages to tell the people. Some of those messages were about Jesus and what would happen to Him in the future. Isaiah told us how Jesus would come to earth. He predicted that someone (John the Baptist) would prepare the way for Jesus to begin His ministry on earth. He said God's Holy Spirit would rest on Jesus, and it did after Jesus was baptized. Isaiah said Jesus' ministry would begin in Galilee. And that happened too. After Jesus was tempted by Satan, He went home to Galilee. The story of Jesus' ministry begins there. It would become the greatest story ever told.

---

*Dear Jesus, it's fun learning more about You. I
can't wait to find out what happens next. . .*

TWELVE DISCIPLES

*"If you keep and obey My Word,
then you are My followers for sure."*
JOHN 8:31

After John baptized Jesus, people began believing Jesus was the Messiah. Some wanted to follow Jesus and learn what He had to say. Jesus chose twelve special followers as His disciples. These men would learn from Jesus and help with His ministry. All but one followed Jesus for the rest of His time on earth. The disciples were Peter, Andrew, James (the son of Zebedee), John, Philip, Nathanael, Matthew, Thomas, James (the son of Alphaeus), Simon, Judas (the son of James), and Judas Iscariot. Jesus' followers weren't only the twelve Jesus chose. He had many followers. You are His follower too if you follow what He taught and believe He is the one who saved you from sin.

Dear Jesus, I am following You when I do my best to behave like You and share what I know about You. . .

MORE PREDICTIONS

Surely the Lord GOD will do nothing unless He reveals His secret to His servants, the prophets.

AMOS 3:7 SKJV

The Old Testament part of the Bible tells the story from when God created the earth until Jesus came. God spoke to many prophets during this time. Among the things He told them were hints about His plan for Jesus and the miracles Jesus would perform here on earth. Isaiah wrote that Jesus would heal people: "Then the eyes of the blind will be opened. And the ears of those who cannot hear will be opened. Then those who cannot walk will jump like a deer. And the tongue of those who cannot speak will call out for joy" (Isaiah 35:5–6). Do you think Jesus' first miracle on earth was to heal someone, or do you think He did something else?

Dear Jesus, because You are God, You can do anything at all. Nothing is too hard for You...

JESUS' FIRST MIRACLE

His followers put their trust in Him.
JOHN 2:11

Jesus and His followers were attending a wedding reception when Jesus' mother, Mary, came to Jesus and said, "They have no more wine" (John 2:3). There wasn't enough wine for all the guests, and Mary knew Jesus could help. Six stone water jars were nearby. Each one held about one-half barrel of water. Jesus said to His helpers, "Fill the jars with water" (John 2:7). So, they filled them to the top. Then He said, "Take some out and give it to the head man who is caring for the people" (John 2:8). They took some water to him. The head man tasted the water and discovered it had become wine! It was better than any wine the guests had tasted. Can you imagine how amazed the people were when they saw Jesus' power? This was the first of many incredible miracles Jesus would perform.

***Dear Jesus, whatever I need, I know
I can call on You for help...***

GOD'S HOUSE, THE CHURCH

If any man destroys the house of God,
God will destroy him. God's house is
holy. You are the place where He lives.

1 CORINTHIANS 3:17

Jesus was in Jerusalem for a special religious gathering. He went into the temple there and found cattle, sheep, and doves being sold. Merchants had set up tables and were selling their livestock for food. The temple is a holy place, the house of God! When Jesus saw it being used as a selling place, He was angry. He pushed the sellers' money off the tables and turned the tables over. He chased the merchants out of the temple, saying, "Take these things out of here! You must not make My Father's house a place for buying and selling!" (John 2:16).

Dear Jesus, whenever I'm in church, I will be respectful. I will remember that I am there as a guest in Your house...

MORE OF GOD'S PLAN

Jesus answered him, "You do not understand now what I am doing but you will later."
JOHN 13:7

After the Jewish religious leaders saw Jesus chase the merchants out of the temple, they said, "What can You do to show us You have the right and the power to do these things?" (John 2:18). Jesus' answer made no sense to them. Jesus said, "Destroy this house of God and in three days I will build it again" (John 2:19). They thought He was speaking of the building. It had taken forty-six years to build the temple. But instead, Jesus was giving them another hint about God's plan: One day, Jesus' body would be destroyed; the people would kill Him. But three days later He would rise from His grave and live again! Jesus often said things people didn't understand. But someday they would see clearly who Jesus was and why He had come.

Dear Jesus, when I read the Bible, please give me understanding so I can know You better...

JESUS KNOWS EVERYTHING

For there is not a word on my tongue,
but behold, O Lord, You know it altogether.
PSALM 139:4 SKJV

God rules heaven and earth. He is all-powerful. That means He controls everything, and He knows absolutely everything that's happening everywhere all the time. He knows even before it happens. Jesus is part of God, so He knows everything too. When He was on earth, Jesus didn't reveal all of God's plan for Him to save us from sin. But Jesus knew the whole plan. He knew that one day He would give up His life for us and that, to everyone's amazement, He would live again. Jesus did many things that showed people He could read their thoughts and even know what would happen before it happened. There was nothing Jesus didn't know.

Dear Jesus, You see everything I'm doing all the time, and You know everything about me. You have my life planned from beginning to end. . .

BORN AGAIN

Jesus said to him, "For sure, I tell you, unless a man is born again, he cannot see the holy nation of God."

JOHN 3:3

A religious leader named Nicodemus asked Jesus about life. Jesus told Nicodemus that to get to heaven, he would have to be born again. Nicodemus didn't understand. Hadn't he already been born? But Jesus was talking about another kind of birth. We all have an invisible part of us called our spirit, or soul. It's the part that gives us our personality and makes us who we are. Jesus said our soul isn't complete until we believe that He is our Savior, the One who saved us from sin so we can live forever in heaven. Believing that makes our spirit whole. Accepting Jesus as Savior makes us part of God's family.

Dear Jesus, if I accept You as Savior, then I will be part of Your family, and one day I will live with You in heaven...

CHILDREN OF GOD

*See what great love the Father has
for us that He would call us His
children. And that is what we are.*

1 JOHN 3:1

God's children aren't just kids. Everyone, no matter how old or young, who accepts Jesus as their Savior is born into God's family right away, and right away Jesus makes a home for them in heaven so it will be ready when they get there. God's family is huge! Imagine how many billions have trusted Jesus as Savior since the time He walked on earth. All of them are in heaven right now. Heaven has no boundaries. It will never run out of space. There is plenty of room there for all of God's children. And in heaven everything is wonderful and perfect. God, our heavenly Father, loves every one of His children, and He has created for them a perfect forever home.

*Dear Jesus, thank You for making a way for me to get
to heaven and creating a place for me there...*

LIVING WATER

"Whoever drinks the water that I will give him will never be thirsty. The water that I will give him will become in him a well of life that lasts forever."

JOHN 4:14

On His way back to Galilee, Jesus stopped in a town called Sycar. Jesus sat resting near a well when a woman came to get water. He asked her for a drink. Jesus knew this woman had done some bad things, and He told her so. Then Jesus said, "If you knew who I am, you would ask Me for living water. Whoever drinks it will never be thirsty again." He spoke in a sort of riddle meaning if she believed He was the Savior, she would forever be forgiven for her sins. At once, the woman knew Jesus was the Messiah. She told others that He had known all about her, and many believed in Jesus because of her.

Dear Jesus, if I accept You as Savior, I will be forgiven for my sins forever. . .

THE SECOND MIRACLE

Trust in the Lord with all your heart, and
do not trust in your own understanding.
Agree with Him in all your ways, and
He will make your paths straight.

PROVERBS 3:5–6

A man met Jesus on the road. He asked Jesus if He would come home with him and heal his son who was dying. But Jesus didn't go with the man. Instead, Jesus said, "Go your way. Your son will live" (John 4:50). So, the man trusted what Jesus said and left. On his way home, the man's friends met him. "Your son is alive!" they said. The man asked when his son had begun to get better, and he discovered it was at the exact moment Jesus had said, "Your son will live." This was Jesus' second great miracle. The man and everyone in his house put their trust in Jesus and followed Him.

Dear Jesus, I don't always understand You, but I will put my trust in You because You are God...

TRUSTING JESUS

When I am afraid, I will trust in You.
PSALM 56:3 SKJV

Can you imagine the man was afraid when he came to Jesus and asked Him to heal his dying son? It seemed there was no hope left for his son. The man was afraid the boy would die. Yet, he hoped Jesus would help. He had heard about Jesus. He believed Jesus was the Savior predicted by the prophets long ago. So the man put his trust in Jesus and went home not knowing what would happen next. That's what Jesus wants us to do—to put our hope and trust in Him, no matter what. The man got what he asked for. But Jesus wants us to learn to trust Him even when we ask and don't get what we want.

Dear Jesus, teach me to put my hope and trust in You and, whatever happens, to keep on trusting You...

NAZARETH

*He said, "A man who speaks for God is
not respected in his own country."*
LUKE 4:24

Not everyone believed Jesus was the Messiah. When He returned to His hometown, Nazareth, He discovered many there did not believe. They had only known Him as Jesus, the son of Joseph and Mary. He had siblings there, and Jesus had grown up in a family like those all around Him. But now He was telling people He was the Messiah, the One God had promised to send to the world to save everyone from sin. He said these things in the temple, and that made some religious leaders angry. They got up and took Jesus out of town to the top of a high hill. They wanted to throw Him over the side. But Jesus got away from them and went on His way.

Dear Jesus, You must have felt sad and alone when the people in Your hometown didn't respect and trust in You...

JESUS UNDERSTANDS

*God has said, "I will never leave
you or let you be alone."*
HEBREWS 13:5

Jesus knows what it feels like to be left out. The people He knew in His hometown had turned against Him, and later many others would too, even some of His closest friends. Maybe you've felt left out or alone. Jesus understands. He understands all your feelings all the time. If you feel sad, lonely, afraid, anxious. . .remember Jesus cares. He loves you, and He says He will never leave you or let you be alone. You can trust Him to stay with you always and to always love you. And Jesus says this: "Do for other people whatever you would like to have them do for you" (Matthew 7:12). If you know someone who feels left out or alone, show them you care. That's what Jesus would do.

---

*Dear Jesus, thank You for always loving me and for
staying with me when I feel lonely, sad, or afraid. . .*

TEACHER

"Follow My teachings and learn from Me."
MATTHEW 11:29

In Galilee, Jesus taught. He shared scripture from the Bible and spoke about living to please God. Jesus was different from the other teachers and religious leaders. He taught as if He had authority greater than any other leader—and He did! He was God's Son, and everything He taught was perfect and true. In Galilee, Jesus did many miracles. He healed those who were in pain. People who hadn't been able to use their legs walked! Jesus healed mental illnesses and all kinds of diseases. The news about Him spread across the country, and many people followed Him. They traveled from city to city, wanting to hear what Jesus said and see what He would do.

Dear Jesus, You've already taught me things I didn't know. Please help me learn even more about You. I want to know what You did and hear what You said. . .

SATAN TRIES AGAIN

*"He speaks with power even to the
demons and they obey Him!"*
MARK 1:27

Satan had tempted Adam and Eve, the first humans. He got them to obey him. Satan had tempted Jesus and tried to get Him to obey too. But that didn't work. Jesus sent him away. Still, Satan was around trying to cause trouble. He sent his demons, his helpers, into the spirit of a man in the temple where Jesus was teaching. The man cried out, "What do You want of us, Jesus of Nazareth? Have You come to destroy us? I know Who You are. You are the Holy One of God" (Mark 1:24). Jesus is more powerful than Satan and any of his demons. He commanded the demons, "Come out of the man!" (Mark 1:25). And they did. The people were amazed by Jesus' power. Even demons obeyed Him.

Dear Jesus, You have power over Satan and any evil thing he tries to do. You rule over everything on earth. . .

JESUS HEALS PETER'S MOTHER-IN-LAW

"Do not fear, for I am with you. Do not be afraid, for I am your God. I will give you strength, and for sure I will help you. Yes, I will hold you up with My right hand that is right and good."

ISAIAH 41:10

Jesus' special friends, His twelve disciples, traveled with Him all the time. They helped Jesus with everything He needed, especially controlling the huge crowd that followed Him around. One day, Jesus went to His disciple Peter's house. Peter's wife's mother was in bed very sick with a high fever. She needed Jesus' help. Jesus went to her, held her hand, and commanded the sickness to leave her. Just like that, she was healed! She felt so well she got out of bed and served Jesus, Peter, and their friends.

Dear Jesus, You are all about everything that is right and good. You are always ready to help us and give us strength...

PETER, ANDREW, JAMES, AND JOHN

God does not change His mind when He
chooses men and gives them His gifts.
ROMANS 11:29

Even before Jesus chose His disciples, He knew who they would be. Each man had already been picked by God to serve Jesus. They were part of His plan, a special team of helpers. Some of the disciples were fishermen. Peter and Andrew were brothers. Jesus saw them fishing and said, "Follow Me. I will make you fish for men!" (Matthew 4:19). Jesus meant He would teach them to find and lead others to follow Him. James and John were also brothers. Jesus found them mending their fishing net. He invited them to be His disciples too. Each disciple was chosen because he had some special skill or talent that would be helpful to Jesus when He traveled and preached.

Dear Jesus, You put together a special team
and each team member had a purpose...

SKILLS AND TALENTS

Every good gift and every perfect gift is from above and comes down from the Father.
JAMES 1:17 SKJV

When God created you, He built into you things you are good at. Maybe there are subjects in school you are good at. Maybe you are strong and athletic, and you play sports well. It might be that you are a super-caring person, and you go out of your way to help others. You could have musical talent or be great at crafts or building. Those special things you do well are gifts from God. He gave them to you to help bring goodness into the world. Think about your special gifts. How could you use your skills and talents in ways that would please God?

Dear Jesus, what are my special skills and talents? Show me. Teach me to use them for good...

MATTHEW AND HIS FRIENDS

*"For I have not come to call good people.
I have come to call those who are sinners."*
MATTHEW 9:13

When Jesus chose Matthew as His disciple, Matthew was working as a tax collector. (Tax collectors weren't well liked back then.) When Matthew invited Jesus to eat with him and his friends, some proud religious law-keepers were upset. Matthew and his friends were sinners—they were known to do things that displeased God. "Why does your Teacher eat. . .with sinners?" the religious men asked the disciples (Matthew 9:11). Jesus overheard them. He said, "People who are well do not need a doctor" (Matthew 9:12). God sent Jesus to earth to save sinners. How could He save them if He sent them away? Jesus welcomed sinners to listen and learn from Him. He wanted everyone to have a place in heaven.

Dear Jesus, we are all sinners. Everyone does things that displease God. You came to save us all from sin because You want everyone to get to heaven. . .

BECOMING MORE LIKE JESUS

But God showed His love to us. While we were still sinners, Christ died for us.
ROMANS 5:8

Everyone is a sinner. We all mess up sometimes. Jesus is the only one who is perfect in every way. When He lived on earth, Jesus didn't turn away those who were imperfect. Instead, He showed them by the way He lived how He wants us to treat one another. Jesus is the best role model. When you change your behavior to be more like His, you will become a good role model too. Jesus loves us, and He wants us to love one another. He forgives us when we mess up, and He wants us to forgive each other too. When you live in ways that please Jesus, you will be showing your family and friends what it's like to follow Him.

Dear Jesus, help me become more like You. I want my behavior to set a good example for others. . .

YOU MUST NOT DOUBT

You must not doubt. Anyone who doubts is like
a wave which is pushed around by the sea.
JAMES 1:6

Jesus was teaching on the shore of the Lake of Gennesaret. The huge crowd pushed against Him. Two boats belonging to the disciples were nearby. So Jesus got in Peter's boat and taught from there. Afterward, Jesus told Peter to take the boat into deeper water and cast his net for fish. The disciples obeyed and took both boats out. They had fished all night and caught nothing. Peter doubted they would catch anything when they cast their nets, but he said to Jesus, "Because You told me to, I will let the net down" (Luke 5:5). When they did, they caught so many fish their nets started to break! The boats almost sank from all the fish inside. Peter knew then that he should always trust and never doubt Jesus.

Dear Jesus, there is no reason to doubt You because
everything You do and say is perfect...

TRUST JESUS

Give your way over to the Lord.
Trust in Him also. And He will do it.
PSALM 37:5

You can always trust Jesus to do exactly what He says. Jesus is God. He is perfect, which means He cannot lie. Lying is sin, and there is no sin in Jesus. When you read about Jesus in the Bible, you can trust that every word written about Him is true. The Bible was given to us by God. He inspired all its words, and what the Bible says is real. When Jesus was on earth, He proved He was the Son of God by doing miraculous things. But He doesn't have to prove anything to us. Jesus is exactly who He was then, God's Son, a part of God. Everything He does is trustworthy, and you can always count on Him.

Dear Jesus, Son of God, I know who You are—You are my friend. You love and care for me, and I know I can trust You. . .

JESUS DOES NOT CHANGE

*Jesus Christ is the same yesterday,
and today, and forever.*
HEBREWS 13:8 SKJV

Everyone and everything on earth changes. Seasons change. So does the weather. Young people grow up and grow old. Daylight changes to night and back to daylight again. Nothing stays the same forever—except Jesus! The Bible says He is the same as He was when He lived on earth, and He will be the same forever. So, when you read about Jesus in the Bible, you can trust that everything He was on earth He is in heaven. That same Jesus you are reading about today is the Jesus you will meet there one day. And when you meet Jesus in heaven, you will know exactly who He is because you learned about Him in the Bible and chose to follow Him.

Dear Jesus, I'm getting to know You a little bit at a time. When I meet You in heaven, then I will know all about You. . .

ALL-POWERFUL JESUS

"So that you may know the Son of Man has the right and the power on earth to forgive sins."
LUKE 5:24

The news about Jesus spread, and the crowds around Him grew. Many came to be healed. Jesus was teaching inside a house where a huge crowd had gathered inside. Men came carrying a man who could not walk. There was no way to get him inside through that crowd. So they made a hole in the roof and lowered the man down. "When Jesus saw their faith, He said to the man, 'Friend, your sins are forgiven'" (Luke 5:20). The man was healed. There was a group of men, proud religious law-keepers, who doubted Jesus was God's Son. They wondered what gave Jesus the right to forgive sins. Of course, Jesus had every right. He had been sent by God to forgive everyone for their sins.

Dear Jesus, You have power over all the earth. You teach us right from wrong and forgive us our sins. . .

PROUD RELIGIOUS LAW-KEEPERS

*Jesus said to them, "See! Have nothing to do
with. . .the proud religious law-keepers and
the religious group of people who believe
no one will be raised from the dead."*
MATTHEW 16:6

The proud religious law-keepers thought they were wiser
than the prophets and those who believed Jesus was the
Messiah. They doubted Jesus was the Son of God, and they
did everything in their power to trap Him. They even got
together to think of ways they could trap Jesus when He
spoke. They wanted to catch Him saying something that
wasn't the truth. But hard as they tried, they weren't able.
And the more they failed, the more they hated Jesus. They
said, "Look, we are losing followers. Everyone is following
Jesus!" (John 12:19). It was these men who would continue
to cause trouble for Jesus, trouble He didn't deserve.

---

*Dear Jesus, no one is wiser than You. No
one is more truthful. No one could ever
prove You aren't the Son of God. . .*

HEALING ON THE SABBATH

*"He who does not honor the Son does
not honor the Father Who sent Him."*

JOHN 5:23

The proud religious law-keepers were critical of anyone who didn't follow God's laws. One law said no work should happen on the Sabbath (the holy day of the week dedicated to God). When the law-keepers saw Jesus healing people on the Sabbath, they said, "Does the Law say it is right to heal on the Day of Rest?" (Matthew 12:10). Jesus answered, "If one of you has a sheep which falls into a hole on the Day of Rest, will you not take hold of it and pull it out? How much better is a man than a sheep! So it is right to do good on the Day of Rest" (Matthew 12:11–12). *Who is this man who speaks as if He is God?* the law-keepers thought. They were so angry with Jesus they planned to kill Him.

---

*Dear Jesus, You are God, and You have
authority to make all the rules. . .*

JESUS CAME FOR THE WHOLE WORLD

*Happy is the nation whose God
is the Lord. Happy are the people
He has chosen for His own.*
PSALM 33:12

Jesus was born in Israel. He was a Jew. The Jewish people were considered God's people because they had a long history with God. When Jesus came to earth, He came to save not only the Jewish people from sin but also everyone else. The huge crowds that followed Him were mostly Jews, but the things Jesus taught were meant for everybody, not just those who lived where He taught and heard Him speak. Jesus' words were written in the Bible so everyone in all the world's countries would know who He is and what He said. Jesus' teachings and His gift of saving people from sin so they could have forever life in heaven were for everyone who would ever live on earth.

---

*Dear Jesus, Your teachings are just as real and
important today as when You lived here. . .*

THE BEST SERMON EVER TOLD

Jesus said to them, "What I teach is not Mine. It is from God Who sent Me."
JOHN 7:16

As word spread about Jesus, He became even more popular. People came from all regions of Israel to see and hear Him. Jesus preached in temples and anywhere people would listen, and He healed every kind of disease and sickness. The people were curious to know more about Jesus. They wanted to hear Him teach. Large crowds came from Galilee, Jerusalem, Judea, and even across the Jordan River. When Jesus saw how many wanted to hear Him, He went up on a mountainside, and He gave them the greatest sermon ever told. The Bible calls it the "Sermon on the Mount." It includes the "Beatitudes"—which means "blessings." Jesus' sermon was about how God wants us to behave.

Dear Jesus, teach me about the kinds of behavior that are pleasing to God...

BLESSED ARE THE POOR IN SPIRIT

*"Blessed are the poor in spirit, for
theirs is the kingdom of heaven."*
MATTHEW 5:3 SKJV

In His Sermon on the Mount, Jesus said those who are poor in spirit will be blessed with the kingdom of heaven. To be "blessed" means to receive a gift from God. Everyone who doesn't know God is poor in spirit. That means their souls have sin inside. We can't get rid of sin on our own, so Jesus came to take our sin away. When He said, "Blessed are the poor in spirit, for theirs is the kingdom of heaven," Jesus was saying those who believe in who He is and that He came to save them from sin would live in God's kingdom, heaven, one day. Heaven is God's gift to those who believe.

Dear Jesus, thank You for blessing me with the gift of heaven. You are the only one who can make my soul clean from sin so I can live there someday...

BLESSED ARE THOSE WHO MOURN

*The Lord is near to those who have
a broken heart. And He saves those
who are broken in spirit.*
PSALM 34:18

The next thing Jesus said in His sermon was "Blessed are those who mourn, for they shall be comforted" (Matthew 5:4 SKJV). He meant that when people are sad, God wants to bless them by coming inside their hearts to love them and help them feel better. The Bible says God loves us. He understands how we feel when we're sad. He even knows how many tears we've cried. God remembers all the times we've felt sad and what caused the sadness. Jesus knows when we feel sad too. You can always trust Jesus to love you and wipe away every tear.

Dear Jesus, when I feel sad, I will remember that I'm not alone. You are with me inside my heart. You understand what sadness feels like, and You will comfort me. . .

BLESSED ARE THE MEEK

*"Blessed are the meek, for they
shall inherit the earth."*
MATTHEW 5:5 SKJV

Some people are so full of themselves they believe they can do everything without God's help. In His sermon, Jesus warned those people. He said the meek would receive a blessing. If you are familiar with the word *meek*, you might think it describes people who never stand up for themselves and always give in. But Jesus taught about a different kind of meek. His definition of *meek* means giving in to God's will. When we give in to God's will, then we want what God wants instead of what we want. Jesus said the blessing for the meek is they will inherit the earth. He meant God would supply them with everything they need.

---

*Dear Jesus, please remind me to be meek before
God and to ask for His will to be done in my life.
Then He will give me everything I need. . .*

FILLED UP WITH RIGHTEOUSNESS

"Blessed are those who hunger and thirst after righteousness, for they shall be filled."
MATTHEW 5:6 SKJV

Think of a time when you felt really hungry or thirsty and all you thought about was getting something good to eat or drink. The fourth blessing Jesus talked about was for those who are hungry to be right with God—those who want to please God as much as they want food and water to fill their bellies. So far you have learned just a little about Jesus, but if, more than anything else, you want to know all about Jesus and please Him through your behavior, then you are hungry and thirsty for righteousness. Righteousness is being right with God. You can never be completely righteous because that would mean you are perfect, like God is. But, still, you can try your best to please Him.

Dear Jesus, if I try to be righteous, You will bless me by making me more like You. . .

BLESSED ARE THE MERCIFUL

"Blessed are the merciful,
for they shall obtain mercy."
MATTHEW 5:7 SKJV

In the Sermon on the Mount, Jesus had already shared four ways to receive blessings. The fifth way, He said, is to be merciful to others. Jesus is merciful. That means He continues to love and forgive us even when we don't deserve it. If we behave like Jesus and love and forgive others when they don't deserve it, then Jesus says we will receive mercy in return. Treating others with mercy shows them what mercy looks like. It might lead them to be more merciful too. We all mess up and need God's forgiveness. But here's something you can count on: whenever you do or say anything that displeases Jesus and you ask for His forgiveness, Jesus will bless you with His mercy—every single time.

Dear Jesus, forgive me when I do things that displease You. Thank You for being merciful to me, and please lead me to be merciful toward others. . .

A PURE HEART

*He who loves a pure heart and is kind in
his speaking has the king as his friend.*
PROVERBS 22:11

Jesus said, "Blessed are the pure in heart, for they shall see God" (Matthew 5:8 skjv). A pure heart is one without sin. It's impossible for humans to have pure hearts because we all mess up. There isn't a person who has ever lived a perfect, sinless life. So, how can we get rid of the sin in our hearts and make them pure? Jesus! His life on earth would end with Him dying to save us from sin. Jesus made it possible for our hearts to be made perfectly pure when we die. With all the sin removed from our hearts, we will be ready to enter heaven and be blessed there to see and live with Jesus.

---

*Dear Jesus, please create in me a pure heart so, someday,
I'll see You in heaven and spend forever with You there...*

BLESSED ARE THE PEACEMAKERS

You are now children of God because you
have put your trust in Christ Jesus.
GALATIANS 3:26

Jesus went on preaching about blessings. Next, He said, "Blessed are the peacemakers, for they shall be called the children of God" (Matthew 5:9 skjv). Are you a peacemaker? You are if you do your best to get along with others. A peacemaker answers calmly and respectfully instead of arguing. Peacemakers do their best to stop fights and arguments from starting. They show mercy and forgiveness to others and do their best to love others even when they seem unlovable. Peacemakers help make the world a better place. Do you know anyone who does those things? Jesus, God's Son! You are God's child too. So do your best to be like Jesus. Bring some peace to the world.

Dear Jesus, I want to be a peacemaker.
If I feel like I'm getting angry or I want to
argue, please help me stay calm. . .

STAND UP FOR RIGHTEOUSNESS

*"Blessed are those who are persecuted
for righteousness' sake, for theirs
is the kingdom of heaven."*
MATTHEW 5:10 SKJV

Jesus finished the blessings part of His sermon by talking about being teased and treated poorly for doing what is right. You already know that being righteous is being right with God. If your goal is to please Jesus by doing what is right, Jesus will see that, and He will bless you. When you stand up for good behavior, those who don't know or believe in Jesus might tease you. It's not fun being teased, but remember you aren't alone. Jesus is with you all the time, and if anyone or anything gets in your way, He will make you strong. Keep being righteous—then Jesus says you will be blessed with all the wonderful things in heaven.

---

*Dear Jesus, I will never be ashamed for behaving
in ways that please You. What others think of me is
far less important than what You think of me. . .*

LOVE YOUR ENEMIES

*"But I tell you, love those who hate you.
(*Respect and give thanks for those who say
bad things to you. Do good to those who
hate you.) Pray for those who do bad things
to you and who make it hard for you."*

MATTHEW 5:44

If people make fun of you for believing in Jesus or for standing up for what you know is right or for any other reason, then Jesus has this advice: pray for them and do your best to think well of them. That's hard sometimes, especially if your feelings are hurt or you feel angry. But if you put more of your thoughts and energy into trying to find the good in others and praying for them, it can help make those feelings of anger and sadness go away. Loving your enemies and praying for them will lead you nearer to God.

Dear Jesus, it's not easy loving and praying for those who hurt me, but with Your help I can do it. . .

SALT AND LIGHT

"You are the salt of the earth....
You are the light of the world."
MATTHEW 5:13–14

The crowd had come to hear Jesus, and as they listened to Him there on the mountainside, they were amazed by what He had to say. He spoke with authority and wisdom. Jesus wanted the people not only to hear His instructions but also to put them into action. "You are the salt of the earth," He said. Salt gives flavor to things to make them taste even better. Jesus wanted His followers to share what He had to say. Doing this would add flavor to the world and make it an even better place. He said His followers were the light of the world. Sharing His words would open the eyes of others to see God. It would lead them out of the darkness of sin.

Dear Jesus, I want to be salt and light for the world.
I will share Your words with my family and friends...

JESUS TEACHES ABOUT ANGER

If you are angry, do not let it become sin.
Get over your anger before the day is finished.
EPHESIANS 4:26

Jesus said that when there is anger, it is important to make right what is wrong. God sees when people argue and are angry with each other, and He doesn't like it. When there is no forgiveness, anger turns into sin. In His Sermon on the Mount, Jesus gave the example of someone getting angry and saying to his friend, "You're a fool!" or "You have no brains!" God hears things like that, and it doesn't please Him. Jesus said it's important to work out your disagreements; then you will be right with God. Think about this: If you and a friend had an argument, what could you do to make things right with each other?

Dear Jesus, sometimes I get into disagreements,
and I feel angry. Please help me learn to work things
out when we disagree. I want us to get along. . .

JESUS TEACHES ABOUT PROMISES

*"You have heard that it was said long ago,
'You must not make a promise you
cannot keep. You must carry out
your promises to the Lord.'"*

MATTHEW 5:33

Jesus spoke to the people about making promises. He said it's important to make promises you know you can keep. When you make a promise to someone, God knows. It's as if you are making that promise to Him. Think about it: If you promise your mom you will clean your room by the time she gets home from work, it is the same as if you made that promise to God. Do you think He would be pleased if you didn't follow through? Jesus said we need to be careful when making promises. He also said we should watch our language when making a promise. Never say things like "Honest to God, I'll do it" or "I swear to God, I'll do it."

Dear Jesus, please help me keep my promises. . .

JESUS TEACHES ABOUT GETTING EVEN

*"But I tell you, do not fight with
the man who wants to fight."*
MATTHEW 5:39

Jesus had strong words for His listeners about getting even. He said, "Do not fight with [someone] who wants to fight." He gave examples to teach the people to avoid a fight at all costs—that means to do whatever is necessary to keep a fight from happening no matter what. Let's give this one some thought: What would you do if a kid at school got angry and started shouting at you, maybe even making fun of you and calling you names? Would you shout back and try to get even, or would you avoid fighting? What might you do to stop the fight?

Dear Jesus, when someone picks a fight with me, show me what to do. I want to keep from fighting, no matter what. . .

JESUS TEACHES ABOUT HELPING OTHERS

"Be sure you do not do good things in front of others just to be seen by them. If you do, you have no reward from your Father in heaven."
MATTHEW 6:1

As Jesus stood on the mountainside preaching, maybe He saw His helpers silently moving through the crowd. His disciples might have been checking in with those listening to Jesus to find out if anyone had a need. Jesus' disciples were learning from Him to help others because it was right and not because they should expect something in return. Jesus said that if you provide help or give to others just so others will see how wonderful you are, you won't please God. Jesus expects you to help whenever and wherever you can only because it's the right thing to do. Then God will see you helping, and He will send blessings your way.

Dear Jesus, thank You for teaching us to be Your helpers and to give without expecting anything in return...

JESUS TEACHES ABOUT PRAYER

*"When you pray, do not be as those who
pretend to be someone they are not. They
love to stand and pray in the places of
worship or in the streets so people can
see them. For sure, I tell you, they have
all the reward they are going to get."*

MATTHEW 6:5

Jesus reminded His listeners to be themselves when they
pray. Praying is more than reciting words of prayers you
read in books or learn in church. Prayer is going someplace
quiet where you can be alone with God. It's telling Him your
feelings and thoughts and asking Him to forgive your sins
and to help you forgive the sins of others. Prayer is about
asking God for what you need. He knows even before
you ask, but still God wants you to talk with Him about
everything. Do you have a quiet place where you can be
alone with God and pray?

---

*Dear Jesus, let's find a place to spend
some quiet time together...*

GATHERING RICHES

"For wherever your riches are,
your heart will be there also."
MATTHEW 6:21

What do you think of when you hear the word *riches*? Maybe your thoughts turn to expensive vacations; designer shoes, clothing, and jewelry; front-row tickets to concerts and sports events; fast cars and big houses with tennis courts, swimming pools, and servants. . . Jesus said to be careful about giving too much importance to such things. He reminded the crowd that all earthly things get worn out, rusty, or even eaten by bugs. He said to gather riches that are worthy of heaven. Things like loving, helping, caring, forgiving, sharing, and bringing peace into the world will last forever; nothing on earth can destroy them. It's those kinds of riches that matter to God.

Dear Jesus, help me shift my focus from the riches here on earth to those that will be remembered forever in heaven. . .

JESUS TEACHES ABOUT WORRY

*"Do not worry about tomorrow. Tomorrow
will have its own worries. The troubles we
have in a day are enough for one day."*
MATTHEW 6:34

Jesus had been speaking for a long while. Maybe He knew that some in the crowd were anxiously worrying about finding something to eat or getting home before dark or putting on warmer clothing as the sun went down. He said, "Do not worry about what you are going to eat and drink. . . . You have so little faith! . . . Do not keep saying, 'What will we eat?' or, 'What will we drink?' or, 'What will we wear?' The people who do not know God are looking for all these things. Your Father in heaven knows you need all these things" (Matthew 6:25, 30–32). Jesus was reminding the people that they didn't have to worry about anything, because God has everything in His control.

*Dear Jesus, whenever I feel anxious or worried,
remind me that You already know what's going
to happen. You will provide what I need. . .*

JESUS TEACHES ABOUT JUDGING OTHERS

"Do not say what is wrong in other people's lives. Then other people will not say what is wrong in your life."
MATTHEW 7:1

It could be that Jesus overheard someone in the crowd getting impatient and grumpy. Maybe unkind words were exchanged. We can't know all of what took place on the mountainside that day. But we do know that Jesus reminded the crowd not to judge one another. Everyone sins. We all get tired and grumpy and say things we don't mean. If we say something unkind to someone and that person says something unkind back, it creates an argument. That sort of behavior doesn't please God. Jesus said we need to judge others fairly and with wisdom. Most of the time, it's best not to judge their behavior at all and leave the judging to God.

Dear Jesus, I don't want to be impatient and grumpy with others or criticize them. Help me remember that I'm just like them—I mess up too. . .

THE GOLDEN RULE

*"Do for other people whatever you
would like to have them do for you."*
MATTHEW 7:12

Jesus taught the crowd many things that day about living to please God. The people were amazed by what He said. Near the end of His sermon, Jesus gave them one rule that would be easy to remember. If they took from His sermon just this one piece of advice, the world would be a better place. Jesus said, "Do for other people whatever you would like to have them do for you." It's called "The Golden Rule." Think about it: How do you want others to treat you? List a few of the ways you want others to behave toward you. Do you always treat others the way you want them to treat you?

---

*Dear Jesus, help me to remember Your special rule and to
do my best to treat others the way I want to be treated...*

"GIVE THEM SOMETHING TO EAT"

*And my God will give you everything you need
because of His great riches in Christ Jesus.*
PHILIPPIANS 4:19

When Jesus finished His Sermon on the Mount, it was evening. The crowd had grown to about five thousand people. They had been on the mountainside for a long while listening to Jesus, and now they were tired and hungry. Jesus' followers came to Him. They said, "This is a desert. The day is past. Send the people away so they may go into the towns and buy food for themselves" (Matthew 14:15). But Jesus said to them, "They do not have to go away. Give them something to eat" (Matthew 14:16). The disciples looked at the huge crowd. There was no food to buy in the desert. How could they feed so many people? It seemed impossible. But—with Jesus everything is possible! What do you think He did?

---

*Dear Jesus, nothing is too hard for You, not even feeding
five thousand people where there is no food. . .*

A LITTLE BOY'S LUNCH

The people saw the powerful work
Jesus had done. They said, "It is true!
This is the One Who speaks for God
Who is to come into the world."
JOHN 6:14

One of Jesus' disciples said to Jesus, "There is a boy here who has five loaves of barley bread and two small fish" (John 6:9). That's all the food there was! Jesus said, "Have the people sit down" (John 6:10). He took the loaves and gave thanks. Then He gave the bread to those who were sitting down. The fish were given out the same way. The boy's lunch multiplied again and again! People had as much as they wanted. When they were done eating, Jesus told His disciples, "Gather up the pieces that are left. None will be wasted" (John 6:12). The followers gathered the pieces, and twelve baskets of leftovers were filled after all the people had eaten.

Dear Jesus, when I think something is
impossible, I will put my hope in You...

JESUS TELLS OF HIS DEATH

Jesus said to them, "But who do you say that I am?" Peter said, "You are the Christ of God."
LUKE 9:20

Jesus' followers believed He was the Messiah, the One who would save us from sin. But they had no idea how He would save us. Jesus shared with them more of God's plan, but He told them not to tell anyone. Jesus said, "[I] must suffer many things. The leaders and the religious leaders and the teachers of the Law will have nothing to do with [Me]. [I] must be killed and be raised from the dead three days later" (Luke 9:22). Then He said, "If anyone wants to follow Me, he must give up himself and his own desires. He must take up his cross everyday and follow Me" (Luke 9:23). What was to come wouldn't be easy for Jesus, or His disciples.

Dear Jesus, following You takes faith. Your disciples didn't know what would happen, and still they chose to follow You. . .

"GIVE US MORE FAITH!"

The followers said to the Lord,
"Give us more faith."
LUKE 17:5

The disciples wanted their faith in Jesus to become even stronger. They asked Him for more faith. But instead, Jesus gave them something to think about. He said, "If your faith was as a mustard seed, you could say to this tree, 'Be pulled out of the ground and planted in the sea,' and it would obey you" (Luke 17:6). A mustard seed is the tiniest of seeds, but when planted, it becomes a huge shrub. Jesus was comparing the seed to growing God's kingdom on earth. When people put their faith in Jesus, that faith takes root in their hearts, and it grows. The disciples had just begun to learn about Jesus. With each miracle He performed, their faith grew. But the best was still to come. Soon, they would see God's plan play out before their eyes, and their faith would become stronger than ever.

Dear Jesus, give me more faith. . .

VISITORS FROM HEAVEN

*"This is My Son, the One I have
chosen. Listen to Him!"*
LUKE 9:35

Jesus took several disciples with Him up on a mountain to pray. While there, something incredible happened. Jesus suddenly looked different! His clothing became white, glowing, and shining bright. Then two men appeared, shining and bright. They were Moses and Elijah, prophets who had lived in the days when the Old Testament was written. They talked with Jesus about His death. The disciples saw this. Then a cloud came all around them, and a voice came from the cloud, saying, "This is My Son, the One I have chosen. Listen to Him!" (Who do you think that was?) The disciples were afraid, and they told no one what they had seen. Do you think they had even more faith after hearing God's voice and seeing Moses and Elijah come down from heaven?

*Dear Jesus, I will listen to Your teaching.
I want to hear Your words. . .*

A MAN WITH GREAT FAITH

*Our life is lived by faith. We do not
live by what we see in front of us.*
2 CORINTHIANS 5:7

An army captain came to Jesus asking for help. His servant was sick and in terrible pain. The captain wanted Jesus to heal him. "I will come [to your house] and heal him," Jesus said (Matthew 8:7). But the captain replied, "Lord, I am not good enough for You to come to my house. Only speak the word, and my servant will be healed" (Matthew 8:8). The man believed in Jesus' power to do anything. He likely had heard of the great things Jesus had done, and he believed that without having to take even one step toward his house, Jesus had power to heal his servant. Jesus said to His followers, "For sure, I tell you, I have not found so much faith in [this whole nation]" (Matthew 8:10). And the servant was healed.

---

*Dear Jesus, You can do anything just
by saying, "Let it be so"...*

HE SPEAKS FOR GOD

*"A great Man Who speaks for
God has come among us!"*
LUKE 7:16

Jesus' popularity was growing. The news of His miracles spread across the land, and crowds followed wherever He went. One day, Jesus arrived at a city where a funeral was happening. As the casket was carried out, a woman walked alongside it, crying. Her only son was dead. Jesus cared. He told her, "Don't cry." Then He put His hand on the casket. The men carrying it stopped. Jesus said, "Young man, I say to you, get up!" (Luke 7:14). The man who was dead sat up and started talking! Everyone gave thanks to God and said, "A great Man Who speaks for God has come among us!" They didn't know yet that Jesus was God's Son. He didn't just speak for God—He *was* God.

---

*Dear Jesus, You say in the Bible, "My Father and I
are one" (John 10:30). This helps me understand
that You are both God's Son and God. . .*

"COME TO ME"

"Come to Me, all you who labor and are heavy-laden, and I will give you rest."
MATTHEW 11:28 SKJV

Jesus saw that people worked hard and had many worries. In some ways, life back then was like it is today. People work hard, they worry, and all that work and worry makes them feel tired. Jesus invited the people to come to Him, follow His teachings, and learn from Him. He wanted them to know that although He had all of God's power, He was also understanding and gentle. Maybe Jesus wanted people to remember what had been written about Him long ago by David, a prophet and king: "Give all your cares to the Lord and He will give you strength. He will never let those who are right with Him be shaken" (Psalm 55:22).

Dear Jesus, when I am overwhelmed, worried, or tired, I will come and spend time with You. I trust You to give me strength and to help me calm down and rest...

JESUS AND THE DEMONS

*Jesus healed those who were sick of many
kinds of diseases. He put out many demons.
Jesus would not allow the demons to
speak because they knew Who He was.*
MARK 1:34

Two men possessed by demons (evil spirits from Satan) stood in front of Jesus. They were angry and violent and wouldn't allow anyone to pass by. "What business do You have with us, Son of God?" they asked. "Are You here to make us suffer?" They saw a herd of pigs nearby at the edge of a sea. "If You are going to cast us out, then send us into the pigs." "Go!" Jesus told them. Suddenly, the demons came out of the men and went into the pigs. The whole herd rushed down a steep bank and into the sea. Those who saw ran away and told many others. The people were so afraid they begged Jesus to go away.

---

*Dear Jesus, You have power over Satan
and every kind of evil. . .*

WHO IS THIS MAN?

The proud religious law-keepers went
out and made plans with the followers of
King Herod how they might kill Jesus.
MARK 3:6

The proud religious law-keepers didn't believe Jesus was the Messiah. They wondered, *Who is this man who raises the dead and casts out demons?* They accused Jesus of working for the devil. They demanded that He give them a sign from heaven, but Jesus refused. Jesus didn't abide by their rules. They saw Him socializing with sinners, something the religious leaders would never do because they were too proud. So their hatred for Jesus grew. Jesus told His disciples, "Have nothing to do with the yeast of the proud religious law-keepers" (Mark 8:15). Yeast is used for making bread. It causes the dough to expand. Jesus was warning His followers that the hatred for Him was growing.

Dear Jesus, You would have nothing to do with the devil.
Every miracle You performed on earth came from heaven...

THEY DOUBTED HIM

*You must not doubt. Anyone who doubts is like
a wave which is pushed around by the sea.*
JAMES 1:6

What people thought about Jesus was changing, and not for the better. He made dead people come alive, cast out demons, and healed diseases. But some doubted it was God doing these things. Maybe Jesus was possessed by the devil. Even members of Jesus' own family doubted Him. Jesus went into a house, and a crowd gathered around Him. They kept Jesus so busy He didn't have time to eat. When Jesus' family heard of it, they went to take Him home. They said, "He must be crazy" (Mark 3:21). Jesus' mother and brothers came and stood outside. They sent for Jesus. But Jesus said, "Whoever does what My Father wants is My brother and My sister and My mother" (Mark 3:35). How do you think Jesus felt when His own family doubted Him?

*Dear Jesus, if I ever doubt You, please
lead me back to You. . .*

PARABLES

*O my people, hear my teaching. Listen to
the words of my mouth. I will open my
mouth in picture-stories. I will tell things
which have been kept secret from long ago.*
PSALM 78:1–2

Jesus used simple stories to teach how God wants us to live.
The Bible calls these stories "parables." Often, Jesus' followers
would listen to one of His stories and not understand what
it meant. But then Jesus explained the meaning, and they
got it! The story itself wasn't important, but the lesson was.
His disciples asked Jesus why He used stories with meanings
that were difficult to understand. Jesus replied that His
stories were meant for those who wanted to learn and not
for others, like the religious law-keepers. "I use stories when
I speak to them because when they look, they cannot see,
and when they listen, they cannot hear or understand. . . .
But God has blessed you, because your eyes can see and
your ears can hear!" (Matthew 13:13, 16 CEV).

Dear Jesus, help me understand Your stories. . .

THE WISE AND FOOLISH BUILDERS

*He was teaching them as One Who has
the right and the power to teach. He did
not teach as the teachers of the Law.*
MATTHEW 7:29

Jesus told a story about two builders who had very different ideas when building their homes. The first builder built his home on a rock. One day, the rain came down, so much rain that things began to flood. A powerful wind came along, but the house on the rock stood strong. The second builder built his house on the sand, and when the rain and wind came, the house fell flat. Which do you think was the wise builder and which was the foolish builder? Jesus explained that the foolish builder is like someone who listens to Jesus' words but ignores them. The wise builder is like the person who becomes strong by listening to Jesus' words and putting them into action. Which kind of builder are you?

*Dear Jesus, lead me to become wise by listening
and putting Your words into action. . .*

THE SOWER

*"Be careful to listen to my words.
Let what I say fill your ears."*
JOB 13:17

Jesus told a story about a farmer planting seeds. Some seed fell at the roadside and birds took it. Some sprouted among rocks; the hot sun caused those little plants to dry up and die. Seed that fell among thorns had no room to grow. Only seeds he planted on good ground became healthy plants that created their own seeds and multiplied. Jesus explained that the seed is God's Word. The devil is like birds who want to steal it. Some people hear God's Word joyfully but move on. They are like plants growing between rock; their joy withers and dies. Those who care more about other things than God's Word are like seeds among thorns with no room to grow. But people who put God's Word into action are like seeds planted on good ground. They grow and even create more seed.

Dear Jesus, please make Your Word grow in my heart...

HIDDEN TREASURE

*"But seek first the kingdom of God
and His righteousness, and all these
things shall be added to you."*
MATTHEW 6:33 SKJV

What if you discovered the world's most valuable treasure hidden in a field? Jesus told about a man who found such a treasure. He didn't say if it was buried or just hidden, so we have to imagine that part. Jesus said the man found a treasure so valuable that he wanted to keep it forever. It was too big and too great to take with him that day. So, what did he do? The man sold everything he had, and he bought the field. Jesus explained that the treasure represents God's kingdom. His kingdom is the greatest treasure of all, and the man recognized its awesomeness. Nothing we have here on earth is more valuable. When we welcome Jesus into our hearts, He promises us a place in His kingdom someday.

Dear Jesus, I treasure You as my Savior and friend. . .

THE LOST SHEEP

*"For the Son of Man has come to
seek and to save what was lost."*
LUKE 19:10 SKJV

Jesus told another story: "What if one of you had one hundred sheep and you lost one of them? Would you not leave the ninety-nine...and look for the one which was lost until you find it? When you find it, you are happy as you carry it back. . . . Then you would go to your house and call your friends and neighbors. You would say to them, 'Be happy with me because I have found my sheep that was lost'" (Luke 15:4–6). Jesus said His story was about people who had turned away from God. He told His disciples, "There will be more joy in heaven because of one sinner who is sorry for his sins and turns from them, than for ninety-nine people right with God who do not have sins to be sorry for" (Luke 15:7).

---

*Dear Jesus, if I turn away from You, please
find me. I want to be with You. . .*

THE GOOD SAMARITAN

*Anyone who loves his neighbor
will do no wrong to him.*
ROMANS 13:10

Jesus told about a man who was robbed and beaten on the road to Jerusalem. He lay there suffering, when a religious law-keeper came walking. He didn't help the man; instead, he kept going. So did another man traveling that way. Then a man from Samaria came along. When he saw the man lying there, he hurried to care for him. He dressed the man's wounds and then he took the man to a place where he could spend the night with people who would watch over him. The Samaritan gave the people money to pay for whatever the man needed. Jesus asked, "Which of the men was a good neighbor to the man beaten by robbers?" The Good Samaritan is the correct answer. Jesus said he is the sort of neighbor we should be.

---

*Dear Jesus, lead me to be kind and caring not
only to my neighbors but to everyone. . .*

THE PRODIGAL* SON

*For by His loving-favor you have been
saved from the punishment of sin....
It is not by anything you have done.*

EPHESIANS 2:8

Jesus told about two brothers. The older worked hard, expecting to earn his father's inheritance**. The younger asked for his inheritance ahead of time. He took it, went away, and spent it having a good time. With nothing left, he ended up getting a job feeding pigs, not earning enough to buy decent food. Filled with shame, the younger brother returned home and asked his father's forgiveness. Not only did his dad forgive him, but he also gave him a welcome-home party! This made the older brother angry. Jesus explained that the older brother was like the religious law-keepers who expected a reward for their good works, but the younger brother was like a lost sinner who had been found. Our heavenly Father loves us always. We don't have to earn His love.

**Dear Jesus, thank You for loving me
always, no matter what...**

* prodigal: someone who spends money wastefully
** inheritance: money left to someone after a person dies

JESUS CALMS THE STORM

*He said to His followers, "Why are you
so full of fear? Do you not have faith?"*
MARK 4:40

It was evening, and Jesus said to His disciples, "Let's take the boat to the other side of the sea." So Jesus and His disciples set sail for the other side. A while later, Jesus was asleep when a bad windstorm came up. The waves were coming over the side of the boat and it was filling with water. The disciples woke Jesus, crying out, "Teacher, do You not care that we are about to die?" (Mark 4:38). Jesus got up and said to the sea, "Be quiet! Be still" (Mark 4:39). At once the wind stopped blowing. There were no more waves. Then He said to His followers, "Why are you so full of fear? Do you not have faith?" (Mark 4:40). The disciples said to each other, "Who is this? Even the wind and waves obey Him!" (Mark 4:41).

Dear Jesus, when I am afraid, I will put my faith in You. . .

JESUS WALKS ON WATER

"You have so little faith! Why did you doubt?"
MATTHEW 14:31

One night, the disciples were in their boat on the water without Jesus. Just before daylight, they saw a figure walking toward them on the water. Imagine how afraid they were. "It's a spirit!" they cried. Then they heard Jesus say, "It is I. Don't be afraid." Peter answered, "If it is You, Lord, tell me to come to You on the water" (Matthew 14:28). Jesus said, "Come!" Peter got out of the boat and walked on the water to Jesus. But when it became windy, he panicked and began to sink. He cried out, "Lord, save me!" Jesus put out His hand and took hold of Peter, lifting him up. He said, "You have so little faith! Why did you doubt?" Then the disciples worshipped Jesus. They said, "For sure, You are the Son of God!" (Mark 14:33).

Dear Jesus, when I feel afraid, I will imagine You lifting me up with Your strong, powerful hands. . .

"GO AND PREACH"

*"You go and preach about the
holy nation of God."*
LUKE 9:60

Everyone was talking about Jesus now. He had become well known for His teaching and miracles. Jesus gave His twelve disciples the right and power to heal people and cast out demons. He sent them out on their own to heal the sick and preach about the kingdom of God—that God reigns as King over heaven and earth. Then Jesus chose seventy more to go two by two and do the same. The seventy were joyful when they came back, saying, "Lord, even the demons obeyed us when we used Your name" (Luke 10:17). Jesus answered, "You should not be happy because the demons obey you but be happy because your names are written in heaven" (Luke 10:20). He reminded them that their power came from God.

*Dear Jesus, please lead me to tell others
about You. I want them to know about God's
kingdom and how to get to heaven. . .*

JESUS VISITS MARY AND MARTHA

*Do not worry. Learn to pray about
everything. Give thanks to God as
you ask Him for what you need.*
PHILIPPIANS 4:6

Jesus left Galilee. On His way to another town, He visited the home of His friends, two sisters named Mary and Martha. While Martha was busy preparing dinner for them, Mary sat at Jesus' feet listening to His every word. This upset Martha. She was doing all the work! "Do You see Mary is not helping me?" she said. "Tell her to help me." Jesus answered, "Martha, Martha, you are worried and troubled about many things. Only a few things are important, even just one. Mary has chosen the good thing. It will not be taken away from her" (Luke 10:41–42). If Jesus came to your house, which would be more important: listening to Him or cooking dinner for Him?

*Dear Jesus, nothing is more important than listening
to You and thinking about Your words. . .*

"LAZARUS, COME OUT!"

*"I am the One Who raises the dead and
gives them life. Anyone who puts his trust
in Me will live again, even if he dies."*
JOHN 11:25

Lazarus, Mary and Martha's brother, was sick. The sisters called for Jesus to come heal him. But Jesus didn't come right away. He had something greater in mind. When Jesus arrived, Lazarus had been dead and buried for four days. Mary came to Jesus, crying, "If You had been here, he wouldn't have died!" Jesus went to the tomb where Lazarus' body lay. Others looked on, whispering, "This Man opened the eyes of the blind man. Could He not have kept [Lazarus] from dying?" (John 11:37). Jesus looked up and said, "Father, I thank You for hearing Me. I know You always hear Me. But I have said this for the people standing here, so they may believe You have sent Me" (John 11:41–42). Then Jesus said, "Lazarus, come out!" And, alive again, Lazarus came out of his tomb.

Dear Jesus, I believe God sent You! . . .

THEY PLANNED TO KILL JESUS

*My children, you must respect the LORD and
the king, and you must not make friends with
anyone who rebels against either of them.*
PROVERBS 24:21 CEV

The proud religious law-keepers had a meeting to talk about Jesus. They didn't believe He was the Messiah, the One God promised to send to earth. They worried about people turning away from the Law, which the religious law-keepers followed. They worried people would follow Jesus instead. They said, "What will we do? This Man is doing many powerful works. If we let Him keep doing these things, all men will put their trust in Him" (John 11:47–48). Caiaphas, the head religious leader, said to them, "Do you not see it is better for one man to die for the people than for the whole nation to be destroyed?" (John 11:50). From that day on, they talked together about how they might kill Jesus.

---

*Dear Jesus, You did nothing wrong. Everything You did
was good. You were teaching people to follow God...*

THE PLOT

"But some of you do not believe."
Jesus knew from the beginning who
would not put their trust in Him.

JOHN 6:64

The time was coming to celebrate Passover, a special day when Jews remember how God saved His people, the Israelites, from slavery in Egypt. The proud religious law-keepers knew many people would come to Jerusalem for the celebration. It was the custom for families and others to gather for a special Passover meal. The proud religious law-keepers stood together in the temple, the house of God, and asked each other, "What do you think? Will [Jesus] come to the special supper?" (John 11:56). They decided to find someone who knew where Jesus was and if He would come to Jerusalem. Then they planned to arrest Jesus.

Dear Jesus, You knew what would happen to
You. You know everything! You could have
run away and hid, but You didn't. . .

MARY WASHES JESUS' FEET

How beautiful on the mountains are the feet of him who brings good news, who proclaims peace, who brings good tidings of good things, who proclaims salvation, who says... "Your God reigns!"

ISAIAH 52:7 SKJV

Jesus was at Mary and Martha's house. It was the custom for guests to be given a bowl of water to wash their feet. (Everyone wore sandals, so feet got dirty.) Mary poured expensive perfume on Jesus' feet and washed them. Then she wiped them with her hair. She knew Jesus was God's Son. She loved, honored, and respected Him. Jesus' disciple Judas Iscariot watched. He carried the disciples' moneybag, and sometimes stole from it. "Why wasn't that expensive perfume sold and the money given to the poor?" Judas asked. Jesus answered, "Leave her alone! She has kept this perfume for the day of my burial. You will always have the poor with you, but you won't always have me" (John 12:7–8 CEV).

Dear Jesus, Mary loved and respected You. I love and respect You too...

JESUS ENTERS JERUSALEM

Everyone in Jerusalem, celebrate and shout!
Your king has won a victory, and he is
coming to you. He is humble and rides on a
donkey; he comes on the colt of a donkey.
ZECHARIAH 9:9 CEV

Jesus traveled to Jerusalem for the Passover celebration. On the way, He told two of His disciples, "Go into the town ahead of you. There you will find a young donkey tied. . . . Let it loose and bring it to Me. If anyone asks you, 'Why are you letting it loose?' say to him, 'Because the Lord needs it'" (Luke 19:30–31). Jesus rode into Jerusalem sitting on the donkey. To show honor and respect, people put their coats down on the road ahead of Him. Others cut palm branches and put them on the road. The crowd shouted, "Greatest One! Great and honored is He Who comes in the name of the Lord!" (John 12:13).

Dear Jesus, even now, Palm Sunday is a
special day when people honor You. . .

LIGHT OF THE WORLD

"I am the Light of the world. Anyone who follows Me will not walk in darkness. He will have the Light of Life."

JOHN 8:12

Jesus spoke to a large crowd. "The hour is near for the Son of Man to be taken to heaven. . . . If anyone wants to serve Me, he must follow Me. . . . If anyone serves Me, My Father will honor him. . . . When I am lifted up from the earth, I will attract all people toward Me" (John 12:23, 26, 32). (He was providing another hint about God's special plan. Jesus would be lifted up and nailed on a cross to die.) Jesus said, "The Light will be with you for a little while yet. . . . While you have the Light, put your trust in the Light" (John 12:35–36). Jesus was saying He was the Light God sent into the world. He was God's Son. But the people didn't understand.

Dear Jesus, You are like a bright light shining on a dark world. Wherever You are there is love and hope. . .

SECRET BELIEVERS

Then Jesus spoke with a loud voice, "Anyone who puts his trust in Me, puts his trust not only in Me, but in Him Who sent Me."
JOHN 12:44

Now, more than ever, Jesus led people to believe He was the One God had sent, the Messiah. He was telling them to believe in and trust Him. Many did, but at the same time, they saw that the religious law-keepers did not. If believers let on that they trusted in Jesus, they could be kept out of the temple, so they stayed quiet about their faith in Him. Even among some of the temple leaders there were those who believed. But they kept it secret. They loved having respect from men more than honor from God. If you had lived back then, what would you have done? Would you have stood up for your belief in Jesus, or would you have stayed quiet?

Dear Jesus, I will never be ashamed to say I believe in You. . .

JUDAS ISCARIOT

They have turned against the LORD and can't be trusted. They have refused his teaching.
ISAIAH 30:9 CEV

Jesus' disciple Judas Iscariot (the one who criticized Mary for pouring expensive perfume on Jesus' feet) had secretly turned against Jesus. He allowed Satan to lead him. Without the other disciples knowing, Judas quietly went to see the proud religious law-keepers who wanted to arrest and kill Jesus. Judas said to them, "What will you pay me if I hand Jesus over to you?" (Matthew 26:15). They said they would give him thirty pieces of silver. Then Judas and the proud religious law-keepers made a plan for Jesus to be arrested at a time when there were no crowds around Him. Of course, Jesus knew everything Judas and the religious law-keepers were doing. Jesus knows everything. What would happen to Him next was part of God's special plan.

Dear Jesus, how did You feel when Your friend turned against You? I would have felt sad. . .

PHARISEES AND SADDUCEES

*"But woe to you, scribes and Pharisees,
hypocrites! For you shut up the
kingdom of heaven against men."*
MATTHEW 23:13 SKJV

When you read about the proud religious law-keepers in your Bible, you might find them called Pharisees and Sadducees (scribes). These were Jewish religious groups in Jesus' time. The Pharisees and Sadducees honored laws that God had given His follower Moses long before Jesus was born. These men had much power and insisted people follow the Law. They also were full of themselves and believed they were better than others. When Jesus came along, He preached a new message, one of forgiveness for the sins people did. He even spent time with sinners! When the law-keepers saw huge crowds following Him, they might have been jealous. They worried Jesus was becoming more powerful than they were. That's why they hated Him. They wanted Him killed before He caused more trouble.

---

*Dear Jesus, You taught people to turn away from sin
but also to be forgiving and to love one another...*

THE LAW

We know that our old life, our old
sinful self, was nailed to the cross with
Christ. . . . Sin is no longer our boss.
ROMANS 6:6

Jesus came to save people from sin. So, what does that mean? Before Jesus, people tried to please God by obeying His rules (His Law about living right). As hard as anyone tried to obey, they messed up because no one can be perfect except God. People asked God to forgive them. They made sacrifices to Him to show they were sorry. They often took their best lamb (livestock was valuable back then and traded like money), killed it, and offered it to God as a sacrifice, a way of showing they were sorry. When Jesus came, He became like a sacrifice for us. His death on the cross made it possible for us to be forever forgiven for our sins.

Dear Jesus, even though I'm forever forgiven, I will still
do my best to behave in ways that please You. . .

THE LAST SUPPER

*"You call Me Teacher and Lord. You
are right because that is what I am."*
JOHN 13:13

Jesus was eating supper with His disciples. He knew the time was near when He would leave earth and return to heaven. Jesus loved His disciples, and as a symbol of His love, Jesus washed their feet. Peter said, "I should be the one washing Your feet!" Jesus answered, "Unless I wash you, you will not be a part of Me" (John 13:8). Although they didn't understand yet, Jesus meant that His death on the cross would wash away their sins. He said, "I have washed your feet. You should wash each other's feet also. I have done this to show you what should be done. You should do as I have done to you" (John 13:14–15). The disciples didn't know Jesus was about to leave them. To them, that last supper was like every other supper they and Jesus had shared together.

Dear Jesus, You loved Your disciples, and You love me too. . .

COMMUNION

"Do this in remembrance of Me."
LUKE 22:19 SKJV

As they were eating supper together and celebrating Passover, Jesus took a loaf of bread. He gave thanks and broke it in pieces. He passed the pieces to His disciples and said, "Take, eat, this is My body" (Matthew 26:26). Then He picked up His cup filled with wine and gave thanks. He passed it to them and said, "You must all drink from it. This is My blood of the New Way of Worship which is given for many. It is given so the sins of many can be forgiven" (Matthew 26:27–28). The disciples didn't understand that Jesus was telling them even more about God's special plan. Jesus' body would be broken and bleeding when He died on the cross. Today in our churches we still take Communion to remember that Jesus died on the cross to save us from sin.

Dear Jesus, I will always remember that Your death on the cross saved us from sin. . .

"DO IT IN A HURRY"

*"You have stayed with Me through all the
hard things that have come to Me."*

LUKE 22:28

His disciples had been with Jesus through the best and worst of times—when everyone seemed to love Him and now when many turned against Him. Jesus said, "One of you is going to hand Me over to the leaders of the country. . . . It is the one I give this piece of bread to after I have put it in the dish" (John 13:21, 26). Then He put the bread in the dish and gave it to Judas. "Go, do it in a hurry," Jesus said. Then Judas went out into the night. The other disciples didn't understand. Judas held the money for them, and they thought Jesus was sending him to buy something for their supper or to give to the poor. They had no idea what would happen next.

---

*Dear Jesus, if I had been one of the disciples, I hope
I would have stayed with You no matter what. . .*

LOVE ONE ANOTHER

*Love is patient and kind, never jealous,
boastful, proud, or rude. Love isn't selfish or
quick tempered. It doesn't keep a record of
wrongs that others do. Love rejoices in the
truth, but not in evil. Love is always supportive,
loyal, hopeful, and trusting. Love never fails!*
1 CORINTHIANS 13:4–8 CEV

Jesus taught His disciples, "You must love each other as I have loved you. If you love each other, [everyone] will know you are My followers" and "'You must love the Lord your God with all your heart and with all your soul and with all your mind.' This is the first and greatest of the Laws. The second is like it, 'You must love your neighbor as you love yourself.' All the Laws and the writings of the early preachers depend on these two most important Laws" (John 13:34–35; Matthew 22:37–40). Why do you think love is so important?

*Dear Jesus, You are all about love. You love us
now and forever. Your love never ends. . .*

"WILL YOU DIE FOR ME?"

*Let the sinful turn from his way, and the
one who does not know God turn from his
thoughts. Let him turn to the Lord, and He will
have loving-pity on him. Let him turn to our
God, for He will for sure forgive all his sins.*
ISAIAH 55:7

Jesus shared with His disciples more of God's plan. He said, "I will be with you only a little while" (John 13:33). Peter said, "Lord, where are You going?" (John 13:36). Jesus answered, "You cannot follow Me now where I am going. Later you will follow Me" (John 13:36). Peter said to Jesus, "Why can I not follow You now? I will die for You" (John 13:37). He was a loyal follower. Peter loved Jesus. But Jesus answered Peter, "Will you die for Me? For sure, I tell you, before a rooster crows, you will have said three times that you do not know Me" (John 13:38). Peter didn't believe this was true. He would never turn against Jesus!

Dear Jesus, help me never to turn against You. . .

JESUS AND GOD ARE ONE

*The Jews tried all the more to kill
Him. . .because He had. . .called God His Own
Father. This made Him the same as God.*
JOHN 5:18

Jesus told His disciples, "There are many rooms in My
Father's house. . . . I am going away to make a place for you.
After I go and make a place for you, I will come back and
take you with Me" (John 14:2–3). Philip said, "Show us the
Father. That is all we ask" (John 14:8). Jesus answered, "Do
you not believe that I am in the Father and that the Father
is in Me? . . . The Father Who lives in Me does His work
through Me. . . . If you had known Me, you would know
My Father also. From now on you know Him and have
seen Him" (John 14:10, 7). Jesus was telling His followers
that He and God were one. Still, they didn't understand.

---

*Dear Jesus, help me understand that
You are an equal part of God. . .*

THE HELPER

*"When the Helper comes, He will show
the world the truth about sin. He will show
the world about being right with God. And He
will show the world what it is to be guilty."*

JOHN 16:8

When Jesus said He was going away, His disciples didn't understand. Then He said, "I will ask My Father and He will give you another Helper. He will be with you forever" (John 14:16). They still didn't understand. Later, after Jesus died and went back to heaven, God would send another part of Himself into the world—the Holy Spirit, the Helper. God, Jesus, and the Holy Spirit are one. The Holy Spirit would be with us forever and help us choose right over wrong. He is with us today. The Holy Spirit is that little voice inside your heart that says things like "Are you sure that's the right thing to do?"

*Dear Jesus, guide me to recognize the Holy Spirit's
voice when He speaks to me in my heart. . .*

TAKE HOPE!

*"Do not let your heart be troubled.
You have put your trust in God,
put your trust in Me also."*

JOHN 14:1

Jesus said, "In a little while you will not see Me. Then in a little while you will see Me again" (John 16:16). His disciples said to each other, "What is He trying to tell us?" (John 16:17). Then Jesus said, "The time is coming, yes, it is already here when you will be going your own way. Everyone will go to his own house and leave Me alone. Yet I am not alone because the Father is with Me. I have told you these things so you may have peace in Me. In the world you will have much trouble. But take hope! I have power over the world!" (John 16:32–33). The disciples understood that Jesus had come from God and soon He would die and return to God. The rest of God's plan was still a mystery.

---

*Dear Jesus, I don't have to worry, because
You have power over the world. . .*

IT IS TIME

*[Jesus] looked up to heaven and said,
"Father, the time has come! Honor Your
Son so Your Son may honor You."*

JOHN 17:1

After supper, Jesus prayed with His disciples. Then He went with Peter, James, and John to a garden nearby. "You sit here while I go over there to pray," Jesus said. "My soul is very sad. My soul is so full of sorrow I am ready to die. You stay here and watch with Me" (Matthew 26:36, 38). Jesus prayed and asked God several times if it was possible for Him not to die in such a horrible way. But then He said, "[Father,] not what I want but what You want" (Matthew 26:39). Meanwhile, His disciples had fallen asleep. Jesus said to them, "Are you still sleeping and getting your rest? . . . The time has come when [I] will be handed over. . . . Get up and let us go. See! The man who will hand Me over is near" (Matthew 26:45–46).

---

*Dear Jesus, You needed Your friends to be there
for You, but instead they fell asleep. . .*

BETRAYED!

Even a friend of mine whom I trusted,
who ate my bread, has turned against me.
PSALM 41:9

There in the garden, in the dark of night, the head religious leaders and the teachers of the Law and the leaders of the people arrived with swords and sticks. Judas Iscariot was with them. Judas said to them, "The man I kiss is the one." Judas went straight to Jesus and said, "Teacher!" and kissed Him on the cheek. Jesus said to them, "Have you come with swords and sticks to take Me as if I were a robber? I have been with you every day teaching in the house of God. You never took hold of Me. But this has happened as [God's Word] said it would happen" (Mark 14:48–49). When Jesus' disciples saw Him arrested, they were frightened, and they ran away.

Dear Jesus, Your friends ran away and left You
alone. But God was still with You. You are part
of Him, and He would never leave You. . .

DARK DAYS LIE AHEAD

*"They will do all these things to you
because you belong to Me. They do not
know My Father Who sent Me."*
JOHN 15:21

God's plan was beginning to unfold. One of the disciples, Judas, had turned against Jesus and had Him arrested. Now the others worried about their own safety. Was Jesus really who He said He was? Jesus had warned them. He told Peter that before the rooster crowed that next morning, Peter would say three times he didn't know Jesus. Jesus had also said that men would hate them for believing in Him. He told His disciples they would be kicked out of the temples. He said, "The time will come when anyone who kills you will think he is helping God. They will do these things to you because they do not know the Father or Me" (John 16:2–3). The disciples were beginning to understand—dark days lay ahead.

---

*Dear Jesus, even today, there are some people
who are against those who believe in You. . .*

WHAT IF?

"If you think it is wrong to serve the Lord, choose today whom you will serve. Choose the gods your fathers worshiped on the other side of the river, or choose the gods of the [people] in whose land you are living. But as for me and my family, we will serve the Lord."

JOSHUA 24:15

If you had been one of Jesus' disciples, what would you have done? They had to choose: Would they continue following Jesus, or would they abandon Him and run away? Choosing Jesus isn't always easy. When times get hard and Jesus leads you toward something unfamiliar and worrisome, like He did the disciples, you might feel like running. But, if you choose Jesus, you can be sure He will lead you through all the hard places, and you will come out on the other side just fine. That's because He is with you. Jesus loves you. He has power over the world.

Dear Jesus, when times are hard, I choose to follow You. . .

THE ROOSTER CROWS

Peter remembered the words Jesus had said to him, "Before a rooster crows, you will say three times you do not know Me." Peter went outside and cried with loud cries.

MATTHEW 26:75

Soldiers tied Jesus' hands and led Him to the head religious leader's house. Peter followed and stood outside the gate. A servant girl who watched the door said to Peter, "Aren't you a follower of this man?" Peter said, "I am not!" Peter was let inside the gate, where the servants had made a fire in the courtyard because it was cold. Peter stood with them getting warm. They said to him, "Aren't you one of His followers?" Peter lied again and said he didn't know Jesus. "Didn't I see you in the garden with Him?" one of them asked. Peter lied a third time and said he didn't know Jesus. And then, just as Jesus said it would happen, the rooster crowed.

Dear Jesus, Peter loved You, but his fear was stronger than his faith. . .

JESUS TAKEN TO COURT

Again the head religious leader asked Him, "Are You the Christ, the Son of the Holy One?" Jesus said, "I am!"

MARK 14:61–62

Inside, the proud religious law-keepers questioned Jesus, trying to find something to charge Him with so they could convince the governor to sentence Him to die. But they found nothing. Then they asked Jesus if He was God's Son, the Messiah. Jesus answered that He was. They covered Jesus' face, and they hit Him. They said, "If You are God's Son, tell us what is going to happen in the future." The soldiers hit Him and spit on Him. The head religious law-keeper said, "You have heard Him speak as if He were God! What do you think?" (Mark 14:64). They all said Jesus was guilty and deserved to die. Then they took Him away to Pontius Pilate, the governor, to be charged and sentenced.

Dear Jesus, You hadn't done anything wrong! You were God's Son, sent to earth to save us from sin. . .

"NAIL HIM TO A CROSS!"

Pilate asked Jesus, "Are You the King of the Jews?" He said to Pilate, "What you say is true."

MARK 15:2

Jesus stood before Pilate, the governor. Every year during the Passover celebration, Pilate let a criminal go free. A crowd had gathered. Pilate said, "Do you want me to let Jesus go free?" The religious leaders had convinced the people that Pilate should free a murderer named Barabbas. "Free Barabbas!" the people cried. Pilate said to them, "What do you want me to do with this man who says He is King of the Jews?" They shouted, "Nail Him to a cross!" Then Pilate said, "Why? What bad thing has He done?" They shouted all the more, *"Nail Him to a cross!"* Pilate wanted to please the people, so he freed Barabbas and had Jesus beaten. Then he sentenced Jesus to be nailed to the cross.

Dear Jesus, they had followed You and listened to Your teaching. Now, they all turned against You. . .

CROWN OF THORNS

*He was hated and rejected; his life was
filled with sorrow and terrible suffering.
No one wanted to look at him. We despised
him and said, "He is a nobody!"*
ISAIAH 53:3 CEV

The soldiers led Jesus away to a large room. They put a purple robe on Him and a crown made of sharp, prickly thorns on His head. "Hello, King of the Jews!" they laughed (Matthew 27:29). Then they hit Him with a stick and spit on Him. They made fun of Jesus, getting down on their knees and pretending to worship Him. Then, after they had made fun of Him, they took the purple robe off Jesus. They put His own clothes back on Him and led Him away, making Him carry the heavy wood cross. Jesus struggled carrying the cross, so when the soldiers saw a man named Simon, from the country of Cyrene, they made him carry the cross for Jesus.

Dear Jesus, You suffered so much to save us from sin. . .

ON THE CROSS

"Father, forgive them. They do not know what they are doing."
LUKE 23:34

Jesus knew what would happen next. It was part of God's plan. It would be terrible and painful, but Jesus was willing. Like those valuable lambs people gave as offerings to God before Jesus was born, Jesus was going to give His own life for us. The people didn't know it yet, but while Jesus was on the cross, all the sin people did—then and forever in the future—would be poured into Jesus. Jesus would take the punishment people deserved for all that sinning. Jesus was willing to do that for us so when we die, all our sins will be washed clean and we will be ready and perfect enough to enter heaven. The soldiers nailed Jesus' hands and feet to the big wooden cross. Then they set the cross upright and left Jesus there to die.

Dear Jesus, You must have loved us so much to take the punishment we deserved. . .

TWO CRIMINALS

*They thought of Him as One Who broke
the Law. Yet He Himself carried the sin
of many, and prayed for the sinners.*
ISAIAH 53:12

Two criminals were also sentenced to die. One was nailed
to a cross on the right side of Jesus, the other on His left.
"If You are the Christ, save Yourself and us," said one (Luke
23:39). The other believed Jesus was God's Son. He said, "Are
you not afraid of God? . . . We are suffering and we should,
because of the wrong we have done. But this Man has done
nothing wrong" (Luke 23:40–41). Then he said to Jesus,
"Lord, remember me when You come into [heaven]" (Luke
23:42). Jesus answered, "For sure, I tell you, today you will
be with Me in Paradise" (Luke 23:43). While nailed to the
cross, Jesus remained gentle and kind. He even asked God to
forgive those who had hurt Him and sentenced Him to die.

---

*Dear Jesus, You suffered on the cross without
complaining or getting angry; instead You
prayed for those who hurt You. . .*

DARKNESS

*Jesus cried with a loud voice, "My God,
My God, why have You left Me alone?"*
MARK 15:34

Those who watched shook their heads and laughed at Jesus.
They made fun of Him and said, "You were the One Who
could destroy the house of God and build it again in three
days. Save Yourself and come down from the cross" (Mark
15:29–30). Others said, "Let [Jesus], the King of the Jews,
come down from the cross. We want to see it and then we
will believe" (Mark 15:32). From noon until three o'clock
it was dark, like nighttime, over all the land. Then, at three
o'clock Jesus cried in a loud voice, "My God, My God, why
have You left Me alone?" All of the world's sin had been
poured into Him, and Jesus knew what it felt like to be all
by Himself and punished for displeasing God. He took the
punishment so we wouldn't have to.

---

*Dear Jesus, thank You for taking the
punishment we deserved...*

JESUS DIES

Then Jesus cried out with a loud voice,
"Father, into Your hands I give My
spirit." When He said this, He died.
LUKE 23:46

Finally, it was finished. Jesus had hung there, hands and feet nailed to the cross, for hours. He had taken on all the world's sin. His whole body was suffering and in pain, it couldn't take any more abuse, and Jesus died. There was a holy place inside the Jewish temple where only priests were allowed to go. A curtain separated that place from the rest of the temple. The Bible says that when Jesus died, the curtain tore in half! The earth shook, rocks fell, graves opened, and many of God's people who were dead were alive again. The soldiers and all those who were watching Jesus saw these things. They felt the earth shake, and they were terrified. They said, "For sure, this Man was the Son of God" (Matthew 27:54).

Dear Jesus, I wonder: Were they sorry
for what they had done?...

WHO WAS AT THE CROSS?

Then all the followers left Him and ran away.
MATTHEW 26:56

Were Jesus' twelve disciples there while He hung on the cross? We don't know for sure, but we can imagine they had left Him. The Bible only tells us that Jesus' disciple John was there. A great many people watched as Jesus died. We know soldiers were there and the proud religious law-keepers. Jesus' mother, Mary, was there along with her sister, also named Mary. And there was a third Mary, Mary Magdalene. She was a special friend to Jesus. While Jesus hung on the cross, He looked down at His mother as she stood next to John. He said to her, "Woman, look at your son" (John 19:26). Then He said to John, "Look at your mother" (John 19:27). From that time on, John was like a son to Jesus' mother, Mary. He took her into his house and cared for her.

---

*Dear Jesus, I wonder: Were the disciples
ashamed for leaving You? . . .*

THINK ABOUT IT

But if a man suffers as a Christian,
he should not be ashamed.
1 PETER 4:16

Jesus' disciples had followed Him wherever He went. They had learned from His teaching and trusted Him. Imagine you were one of His disciples when Jesus was arrested and taken away. It seemed everyone had turned against Jesus. They hated Him and wanted Him killed. Would you worry that they would turn against you, too, for being a Jesus follower? That was the problem the disciples faced. What do you think you would have done? Would you have followed Jesus, no matter what? Today, we call people who believe in Jesus and follow His teaching "Christians." It isn't always easy being a Christian. There are still those in the world who hate Jesus. But true Christians are never ashamed to say they know Jesus and love Him. They trust in Jesus, no matter what.

Dear Jesus, help me hold on to my trust
in You so I won't ever leave You. . .

THEY BURIED HIM

"When everything was done that had been written about Him, they took Him down from the cross and laid Him in a grave."
ACTS 13:29

Joseph, a man from a city called Arimathea, was a follower of Jesus. He was afraid of the proud religious law-keepers, so he worshipped Jesus without anyone knowing. Without being afraid, Joseph went to Pilate and asked for Jesus' body. Then Joseph took Jesus' body, wrapped it in linen cloth, and put it inside his own tomb, a place that had been cut out of the side of a huge rock. He pushed a big stone over the door of the grave and went away. Mary Magdalene and the other Mary were there watching. It was Friday evening. The next day, Saturday, was a holy day of rest. The Marys went home to get spices and perfumes ready so they could come back on Sunday to put them in Jesus' tomb.

Dear Jesus, it was generous of Joseph to give You his tomb...

WHAT WERE THEY THINKING?

From that time on Jesus began to tell His followers that He had to go to Jerusalem and suffer many things. These hard things would come from the leaders and from the head religious leaders of the Jews and from the teachers of the Law. He told them He would be killed and three days later He would be raised from the dead.

MATTHEW 16:21

Wherever they were, Jesus' disciples must have been wondering what would happen next. God's special plan was unfolding before their very eyes. Everything Jesus had said would happen was coming true. Jesus had told His disciples several times that He would suffer because of the proud religious law-keepers. He said He would be killed. Now, those things had happened. But Jesus had also said that after three days He would be raised from the dead. Do you think the disciples believed that would happen too?

Dear Jesus, I wonder where Your disciples were and what they were thinking. . .

GUARDS AT THE TOMB

*So they sealed it tight and placed
soldiers there to guard it.*

MATTHEW 27:66 CEV

The day after Jesus was killed, the head religious leaders
and the proud religious law-keepers went to Pilate. They
said, "Sir, we remember what Jesus, the liar, said when He
was living, 'After three days I will rise from the dead.' Give
us permission to have His grave watched. We are worried
that His loyal followers will come at night and take His
body away and then say to the people, 'He has been raised
from the dead.' It would be a mistake to allow such a thing
to happen." Pilate answered them, "Take the soldiers and let
them watch the grave." So, the proud religious law-keepers
ordered the soldiers to stand by the grave. They made sure
to seal the big stone door so it couldn't be moved.

*Dear Jesus, they still didn't believe You were God's
Son. Would they ever believe in You?...*

HE IS RISEN!

We know that Christ was raised from the dead. He will never die again. Death has no more power over Him.

ROMANS 6:9

Early on Sunday morning, the two Marys went to Jesus' tomb to put spices on His body. Just then, an angel appeared. His face was bright like lightning and His clothes white as snow. The guards at the tomb were so afraid they fell down and passed out. The angel said to the women, "Do not be afraid. I know you are looking for Jesus. . . . He is not here! He has risen from the dead as He said He would" (Matthew 28:5–6). The angel pushed open the stone-sealed tomb, and the two Marys went inside. Jesus' body was gone! "Run fast," said the angel. "Tell His followers that He is risen from the dead. He is going before you to. . .Galilee. You will see Him there" (Matthew 28:7). So they ran in a hurry from the tomb to tell His followers the news.

Dear Jesus, nothing could stop You, not even death. . .

HOLY WEEK

*He died once but now lives. He died to
break the power of sin, and the life He
now lives is for God. You must do the
same thing! Think of yourselves as dead
to the power of sin. But now you have new
life because of Jesus Christ our Lord.*

ROMANS 6:10–11

Each year, Christians celebrate Holy Week. On Holy Thursday, sometimes called "Maundy Thursday," we remember the last supper when Jesus offered the first Communion to His disciples. Good Friday is when we remember Jesus' death on the cross. On Holy Saturday, Christians wait for Easter Sunday—also called "Resurrection Sunday." On that day, we joyfully celebrate Jesus rising from the dead and becoming fully alive again, just as He said He would. We celebrate Him as our Savior, the Messiah who came to save us from the punishment we deserved for our sins. How do you and your family celebrate Holy Week?

*Dear Jesus, Your story seems to have a
happy ending—but is there more? . . .*

FOOLISH TALK

Then Jesus said to them, "You foolish men. How slow you are to believe what the early preachers have said."
LUKE 24:25

The Marys ran off to share the news about what happened. They told their women friends, who hurried to tell others. Then they rushed to tell Jesus' eleven remaining disciples that His body was gone. Where was the twelfth disciple, Judas Iscariot, the one who betrayed Jesus? He was dead. He had taken his own life after he realized the terrible thing he had done to Jesus, his Lord and friend. The women's words sounded like foolish talk to the disciples. They didn't believe them. Peter was the only one who went to the tomb. There, he saw the linen cloths Jesus' body had been wrapped in, but there was no body. He went away, surprised.

Dear Jesus, You taught them to trust in You. Everything the ancient prophets had predicted had happened. Still, Your disciples didn't believe You had risen from the dead. . .

THE BIG LIE

*If a ruler listens to lies, all who work
for him will become sinful.*
PROVERBS 29:12

After the angel had left the tomb and the guards woke up, some of them went to the city to tell the religious leaders everything that had happened. The leaders held an emergency meeting with the soldiers, and they talked about what to do. It was decided that the leaders would pay the soldiers to lie. They gave them a great amount of money to keep quiet about the truth. Then the leaders told the soldiers, "Tell the people, 'His followers came at night and took His body while we were sleeping.' We will see that you do not get into trouble over this if Pilate hears about it" (Matthew 28:13–14). So, the soldiers took the money and lied. This lie was told among the Jews back then and it is still told today.

*Dear Jesus, it is never right to lie. Eventually,
the truth will come out. . .*

WOULD YOU BELIEVE?

If you say with your mouth that Jesus is Lord, and believe in your heart that God raised Him from the dead, you will be saved from the punishment of sin.
ROMANS 10:9

Imagine yourself as one of Jesus' disciples back then, hiding, worried about your own safety. The Marys come rushing to find you. They share a wild story about an angel appearing at Jesus' tomb, soldiers falling to the ground like dead men, the angel easily breaking the seal and moving the stone to reveal that Jesus' body is—gone! Mary Magdalene tells you that after she left the tomb, she saw Jesus and talked with Him. The women say Jesus met them on the road and said hello and told them, "Tell My followers to go to Galilee. They will see Me there" (Matthew 28:10). Would you have believed their incredible story, or would you have decided it was foolishness?

Dear Jesus, without proof, their story sounds too good to be true. I hope I would have believed. . .

PROOF

*We give honor and thanks to the
King Who lives forever.*
1 TIMOTHY 1:17

Jesus' disciple Simon and another follower were walking home and talking about what the Marys had told them. A stranger came and walked alongside them. (It was Jesus, but He looked different. They didn't recognize Him.) They told Him everything that had happened. "You foolish men," Jesus said. "Don't you believe what the early preachers said?" Then Jesus reminded them of everything that had been written about Him by the prophets. When they arrived in their town, the followers asked Jesus to stay with them. He sat with them at the supper table, broke bread into pieces, gave thanks, and shared it with them just as He had done at the Last Supper. Suddenly, their eyes were opened, and they knew Him. Then, just like that, Jesus disappeared! Simon and his friend left at once and hurried to tell the other disciples.

---

*Dear Jesus, their faith wasn't very strong.
They had to see You to believe. . .*

FOR SURE!

They said, "For sure the Lord is risen."
LUKE 24:34

Simon and his friend found ten of the eleven disciples. They told them what had happened on the road and how they had recognized Jesus after He broke the bread, gave thanks to His Father, and shared it with them. "For sure the Lord is risen," they said. As the disciples talked, Jesus came and stood with them. He said, "May you have peace" (Luke 24:36). They were afraid, thinking they saw a spirit. "Why are you afraid?" Jesus said. "Why do you have doubts. . . ? Look at My hands and My feet. See! It is I, Myself! Touch Me and see for yourself. A spirit does not have flesh and bones as I have" (Luke 24:38–39). Then, Jesus showed them His hands and feet. The disciples still wondered. It was hard for them to believe it, and yet seeing Jesus made them happy.

Dear Jesus, what would it take before they truly believed You had risen from the dead? . . .

DOUBTING THOMAS

Jesus said to him, "Thomas, because you have seen Me, you have believed. Blessed are those who have not seen and yet have believed."

JOHN 20:29 SKJV

Jesus' disciple Thomas wasn't with the others when Jesus came. Later, the other disciples told him, "We have seen the Lord!" But Thomas said, "Unless I see the nail marks in Jesus' hands and put my finger where the nails were, and unless I put my hand to His side where they stuck Him with a spear, I won't believe." A week later, all the disciples including Thomas were together in a house. Though the doors were locked, Jesus came and stood with them and said, "Peace be with you!" Then He said to Thomas, "Put your finger here; see My hands. Reach out your hand and put it to My side. Stop doubting and believe." Thomas said to Him, "My Lord and my God!"

Dear Jesus, finally, all the disciples saw You and truly believed You had risen from the dead. . .

SPECIAL INSTRUCTIONS

He said to them, "You are to go to all the world
and preach the Good News to every person."
MARK 16:15

Jesus said to His disciples, "Remember what I told you while I was with you. Everything written about Me by the prophets [in the Bible's Old Testament] must happen as they said." When Jesus said this, He opened their minds to understand everything the ancient prophets had written. Then He continued, "It was written that I would suffer and be raised from the dead after three days. Now it must be preached to the world that everyone should be sorry for their sins and turn from them. Then they will be forgiven. You are to tell everything you have seen. I will send you the Holy Spirit, but you are to stay in Jerusalem until you have received this power from above" (see Luke 24:44–49).

Dear Jesus, now they understood. They
knew it was You speaking to them...

JESUS GOES BACK TO HEAVEN

"He will be with you. He will be faithful to you and will not leave you alone."
DEUTERONOMY 31:8

For forty days, people saw Jesus. He continued teaching His disciples. As they listened to Him, He told them again, "Do not leave Jerusalem. Wait for what the Father has promised. In a few days you will receive the Holy Spirit. You will have special power when He comes into your life. Then you will tell about Me to the ends of the earth" (see Acts 1:4–5, 8). When Jesus finished speaking, the disciples watched as He was taken up to heaven. A cloud carried Him straight up into the sky. Two angels dressed in white appeared. They said, "Why do you stand looking up into heaven? This same Jesus Who was taken from you into heaven will return in the same way you saw Him go" (Acts 1:11).

Dear Jesus, You didn't leave us. Although we can't see You, Your Spirit is with us all the time. . .

THE END OF THE STORY?

*Christ lives in me. The life I now live in
this body, I live by putting my trust in
the Son of God. He was the One Who
loved me and gave Himself for me.*
GALATIANS 2:20

Is this the end of Jesus' story? No. It's the beginning of a new chapter. Jesus went to heaven and took His place on His throne next to God. Just like God, Jesus is a Spirit. We can't see Him, but He is totally with us all the time. The Bible says that if you are sorry for your sins and you believe Jesus died to take the punishment you deserve for displeasing God, then His Spirit will come and live inside your heart forever. Someday Jesus is coming back to earth. People will see Him. He is coming back to get rid of Satan and sin forever.

---

*Dear Jesus, so You went back to heaven to be with
God. I wonder—what happened to the disciples?...*

THE UPPER ROOM

And being assembled together with them,
He commanded them that they should
not depart from Jerusalem but wait for
the promise of the Father. "Which," He
said, "you have heard from Me."

ACTS 1:4 SKJV

In Jerusalem, the eleven disciples found a place to stay in an upper room on the second floor. Jesus' mother, Mary, and His brothers were also with them. Peter talked about Judas, who had betrayed Jesus. He reminded the disciples that this was foretold in the book of Psalms. It said there, "Let another person take over his work" (Psalm 109:8). Peter said, "The man to take the place of Judas should be one who was with us all along and was with us to the day Jesus was taken up to heaven" (see Acts 1:21). The disciples prayed and chose a man named Matthias. From that day on, the twelve disciples would become missionaries, sharing with the world the good news about Jesus.

Dear Jesus, I wonder if the disciples felt alone
and unsure of themselves without You. . .

145

HOLY SPIRIT

"Jesus has been lifted up to God's right side. The Holy Spirit was promised by the Father. God has given Him to us. That is what you are seeing and hearing now!"

ACTS 2:33

Jesus had promised to send the Helper, the Holy Spirit, to His disciples. In the upper room, it happened. A sound from heaven, like a powerful wind, filled the house. Then something that looked like flaming tongues that were split down the middle landed on each of the disciples. All at once, their hearts were filled with the Holy Spirit. They were overwhelmed with God's power and love. They began telling about Jesus in foreign languages that none of them had known how to speak. At that time, people from many other countries were in Jerusalem, and they wondered what in the world was going on with the disciples. They decided Jesus' followers must be drunk.

Dear Jesus, Your Holy Spirit filled the disciples with overwhelming joy and the power to do amazing things. . .

PETER SPEAKS

"Yes, on those I own, both men and women, I will send My Spirit in those days. They will speak God's Word."
ACTS 2:18

Peter stood up and spoke in a loud voice to the people in Jerusalem: "I want you to know what is happening. So listen to what I am going to say. These men are not drunk as you think. . . . The early preacher Joel said this would happen. God says, '. . .I will send My Spirit on all men. Then your sons and daughters will speak God's Word. . . .' The Holy Spirit was promised by the Father. God has given Him to us. That is what you are seeing and hearing now! . . . [You all] must know for sure that God has made this Jesus, both Lord and Christ. He is the One you nailed to a cross!" (Acts 2:14–17, 33, 36).

Dear Jesus, Peter wasn't afraid anymore to stand up and tell others about You. . .

WHAT SHOULD WE DO?

*When the Jews heard this, their hearts
were troubled. They said to Peter. . .
"Brothers, what should we do?"*
ACTS 2:37

Those listening to Peter were afraid. They understood now that they had murdered the real Messiah, the One God had promised all along to send them. They had sinned—big-time! "What should we do?" they asked. Peter told them, "Be sorry for your sins. . .and be baptized in the name of Jesus Christ, and your sins will be forgiven. You will receive the gift of the Holy Spirit. This promise is to you and your children. It is to all people everywhere" (Acts 2:38–39). Peter said many other things. He helped them understand that they should stay away from sinful people. Those who believed Peter were baptized. There were about three thousand more followers added that day.

---

*Dear Jesus, wow, three thousand more followers! Finally,
more people believed the truth that You were really
the Messiah, God's Son, and part of God Himself. . .*

THE FIRST CHURCH

The Lord added to the group each
day those who were being saved
from the punishment of sin.
ACTS 2:47

The disciples had a new role. They were teachers, teaching others what they had learned from Jesus. Soon, many more chose to follow Jesus. They worshipped together, prayed, and shared Communion, just as the disciples had with Jesus at the Last Supper. Many shared what they owned. Some sold everything they had and shared with everyone. Day after day, these new Christians (those who believed in Jesus) went to the place of worship together. This became the first church—a meeting place for Jesus' followers. The number of His followers grew. Many became missionaries. They traveled all across the land telling others the good news—that Jesus had come to save them from sin and promise them forever life in heaven.

Dear Jesus, if I share the good news,
then I'm a missionary too!...

NOT AN EASY LIFE

*"God has raised up His Son Jesus. . .
to give God's favor to each of you who
will turn away from his sinful ways."*
ACTS 3:26

One day, Peter and John met a man who couldn't walk. Peter said, "In the name of Jesus, get up!" The Holy Spirit had given the disciples power to do miracles. Peter took the man by the right hand and lifted him up. At once his legs became strong. He jumped up and walked. There were still proud religious leaders who didn't believe in Jesus. They were angry because Jesus' disciples were performing miracles and preaching that Jesus had been raised from the dead. They put John and Peter in prison for a while. Life wasn't going to be easy for the disciples. The unbelievers would give them plenty of trouble. Still, the disciples never gave up. They continued sharing the good news.

*Dear Jesus, good for Your disciples!
They stayed loyal to You. . .*

THE BIBLE

*No part of the Holy Writings came long
ago because of what man wanted to
write. But holy men who belonged to God
spoke what the Holy Spirit told them.*
2 PETER 1:21

The Bible is made up of many separate books. It is divided into the Old Testament and the New Testament. The Old Testament tells of the time before Jesus was born. Some of it was written by prophets God spoke to. They shared what God said would happen in the future, and especially about Jesus. The New Testament is divided too. The first four books (Matthew, Mark, Luke, and John) tell about Jesus' life here on earth. The rest were written by Jesus' followers who were missionaries after Jesus went back to heaven. The last book tells us that Jesus is coming back to earth one day. Everyone will see Him. His purpose will be to do away with Satan and sin forever.

Dear Jesus, the Bible is one way You speak to us. . .

A NEW FOLLOWER

*"Saul, Saul, why are you working
so hard against Me?"*
ACTS 9:4

Many of the New Testament books were written by a Jesus follower named Paul. His story is interesting. At one time, Paul was known as Saul, and he hated anyone who followed Jesus. In fact, Saul wanted all of Jesus' followers killed. He planned to go to a city called Damascus. But before he left Jerusalem, Saul went to the religious leaders and got letters saying he could arrest and bring back any Jesus followers he found there. On the road to Damascus, a light from heaven shone all around Saul. He fell to the ground. Then he heard a voice say, "Saul, Saul, why are you working so hard against Me?" Saul answered, "Who are You?" The voice answered, "I am Jesus, the One Whom you are working against" (Acts 9:5).

---

*Dear Jesus, how amazing—Saul didn't see You, but he heard
Your voice. You were all around him in that bright light...*

JESUS CHOOSES SAUL

The Lord said to him, "Go!
This man is the one I have chosen."
ACTS 9:15

Saul opened his eyes and discovered that he was blind. He couldn't see, and he was afraid. Jesus sent him to a friend's home in Damascus and told him to wait there. Then Jesus spoke to one of His followers, a man named Ananias. He told Ananias to go to Saul and heal his eyes so he would see again. "But Lord," said Ananias, "many people have told me about this man. . . . He came here with the right and the power. . .to put everyone in chains who call on Your name" (Acts 9:13–14). Then Jesus said to him, "Go! [Saul] is the one I have chosen to carry My name among the people who are not Jews and to their kings and to Jews" (Acts 9:15). So, Ananias went to find Saul.

Dear Jesus, You gave Ananias courage. He was afraid
of Saul; still he did exactly what You told him to do. . .

JESUS SPEAKS TO US

And behold, the LORD passed by, and a great and strong wind tore the mountains. . .but the LORD was not in the wind. And after the wind there was an earthquake, but the LORD was not in the earthquake. And after the earthquake there was a fire, but the LORD was not in the fire. And after the fire a still small voice.
1 KINGS 19:11–12 SKJV

After Jesus returned to heaven, He still communicated with His followers. Most often, He spoke to them inside their hearts in "a still, small voice." (They heard His voice in their thoughts.) You can hear Jesus' voice in your heart too. He is the one who tells you the right things to do and leads you nearer to God. The more you study about Him in your Bible, the easier it becomes to know His voice when you hear it in your heart.

Dear Jesus, please help me recognize Your voice speaking to me in my thoughts. . .

SAUL BECOMES A CHRISTIAN

Follow my way of thinking as I follow Christ.
1 CORINTHIANS 11:1

Ananias found Saul staying at a friend's home in Damascus. Ananias put his hands on Saul and said, "[Jesus] has sent me so you might be able to see again and be filled with the Holy Spirit" (Acts 9:17). At once, something like a covering fell from Saul's eyes and he could see. Soon, he was baptized. Before long, Saul (now known as Paul) began preaching, telling the Jews that Jesus is the Son of God. All who heard him were surprised. They said, "This is the man who beat and killed [Jesus'] followers in Jerusalem. He came here to tie the followers in chains and take them to the head religious leaders" (Acts 9:21). Jesus kept on giving Paul power. This new follower was proving to others that Jesus was the Christ, the Son of God.

Dear Jesus, You can do anything! You turned Saul's life around from hating You to becoming Your follower. . .

PAUL, FOLLOWER OF CHRIST

*I want you to know that what has happened
to me has helped spread the Good News.*
PHILIPPIANS 1:12

Of all the followers after Jesus went to heaven, Paul is probably the most famous. Nothing stopped him from sharing the good news about Jesus. Those who hated Jesus wanted to kill Paul, but he wasn't afraid. He was arrested and put in prison, and even that didn't stop him. Paul traveled to other countries. He made friends there and helped them set up churches. From prison Paul wrote letters to his friends reminding them of what Jesus had said. Paul became a great teacher of God's Word. He believed that all the bad things he'd suffered made him an even stronger Christian. Paul wrote thirteen New Testament books: Romans, First and Second Corinthians, Galatians, Ephesians, Philippians, Colossians, First and Second Thessalonians, First and Second Timothy, Titus, and Philemon.

*Dear Jesus, I want to read Paul's books to
learn more about him and You...*

PAUL'S TROUBLES

*[Jesus said,] "In the world you will
have much trouble. But take hope!
I have power over the world!"*
JOHN 16:33

Paul faced unending trouble while sharing the good news. He wrote a letter telling his friends what had happened to him. "I've been in prison, whipped, and beaten. I've almost died. I was on ships that were wrecked. I spent a day and a night in the water. I've been in danger from high water, from robbers, and from people who don't know God. I've been in danger in cities, in the desert, and on the sea. I've worked hard, been tired, and been in pain. I've gone many times without sleep. I've been hungry, thirsty, and out in the cold. If I must talk about myself, I will do it about the things that show how weak I am" (see 2 Corinthians 11:23–30). Paul reminded his friends that he kept going because of the strength he received from Jesus.

Dear Jesus, Paul must have loved You to suffer so much. . .

FAITH IN JESUS MAKES US STRONG

*Then Jesus said to them, "Do you
have faith that I can do this?"
They said to Him, "Yes, Sir!"*
MATTHEW 9:28

In a letter from prison, Paul reminded his friends, "You have never been tempted to sin in any different way than other people. God is faithful. He will not allow you to be tempted more than you can take. But when you are tempted, He will make a way for you to keep from falling into sin" (1 Corinthians 10:13). Think about it: When Jesus lived on earth, He proved He was a part of God with all of God's power. Jesus can do anything. When you have faith in Him to help you, Jesus will make you strong. Satan will often try to get you to do things you know you shouldn't. When that happens, call on Jesus for help. He will keep you from falling into Satan's trap.

Dear Jesus, when I am weak, You will help me be strong. . .

PAUL'S THOUGHTS ON FORGIVENESS

[Jesus said we should pray:] "Forgive us our
sins as we forgive those who sin against us."
MATTHEW 6:12

Paul had been hurt badly, yet he remembered what Jesus had said. Paul wrote to his friends, "When someone does something bad to you, do not pay him back with something bad. Try to do what. . .is right and good. As much as you can, live in peace with [others]. . . . Let the anger of God take care of the other person" (Romans 12:17–19). Paul added, "[The Lord says], 'I will pay back to them what they should get. . . .' If the one who hates you is hungry, feed him. If he is thirsty, give him water. If you do that, you will be making him more ashamed of himself'" (Romans 12:19–20). Paul reminded them, "Do not let sin have power over you. Let good have power over sin!" (Romans 12:21).

Dear Jesus, Paul suffered so much, but still he
obeyed Jesus and was forgiving. Will You help
me be forgiving, the way Paul was? . . .

PAUL TEACHES ABOUT LOVE

[Jesus said,] "A new commandment I give to you, that you love one another; as I have loved you.... By this [will] all men know that you are My disciples."
JOHN 13:34–35 SKJV

Jesus said, "Love one another." Paul explained what love is. He said, "Love does not give up. Love is kind. Love is not jealous. Love does not [care about] being important. Love has no pride. Love does not do the wrong thing. Love never thinks of itself. Love does not get angry. Love does not remember the suffering that comes from being hurt by someone. Love is not happy with sin. Love is happy with the truth. Love takes everything that comes without giving up. Love believes all things. Love hopes for all things. Love keeps on in all things. Love never comes to an end" (1 Corinthians 13:4–8). Think about it: If you do your best to be loving, you are teaching others to please Jesus. Your loving behavior becomes a good role model for them.

Dear Jesus, teach me to love others the way You love me...

EVERYONE SHOULD PRAY

You must pray at all times as the
Holy Spirit leads you to pray. Pray
for the things that are needed.
EPHESIANS 6:18

Paul prayed for his friends. He asked his friends to pray for him too. Paul asked them to pray that he would find the right words to say when he shared the good news about Jesus. Paul asked God to help his friends learn more about Jesus and know Him better. He asked God to show his friends that Jesus' love is great and more wonderful than anything humans can understand. Paul wanted his friends to have hope and to recognize Jesus' great power. He asked God to make his friends' faith strong and to fill their hearts with love. Do you pray for your friends? Have you ever asked a friend to pray for you?

Dear Jesus, show me how to pray for others. Open my
eyes and heart to recognize what they need. . .

WHAT ARE YOU PRAYING FOR?

*"Your Father knows what you
need before you ask Him."*
MATTHEW 6:8

Jesus taught us to give honor to God when we pray and to ask Him to provide us with everything we need each day. Jesus taught us to ask God to help us do what's right, to lead us away from sin, and to help us be forgiving of those who hurt us. When you pray and ask God for something, you can be sure He will answer. If God agrees with what you pray for, you will receive it. It might not happen right away. God will provide it when the time is right. If what you pray for isn't what God wants for you, He won't give it to you. That's because He knows what's best for you. When you pray, ask Jesus to lead you toward asking for what you need.

---

*Dear Jesus, help me remember that what I want
isn't always what God knows I need. . .*

PAUL TEACHES ABOUT PRIDE

*[Jesus said:] God blesses those people
who depend only on him. They belong
to the kingdom of heaven!*
MATTHEW 5:3 CEV

Being humble means not thinking of yourself as more important than anyone else. Paul reminded his friends to be humble the way Jesus was. He told his friends, "Nothing should be done because of pride or thinking about yourself. Think of other people as more important than yourself" (Philippians 2:3). Jesus put the needs of others before His own. Jesus never was prideful or boasted about all the good things He did. Often after He healed someone or did other miracles, Jesus gave thanks to His Father. That's what we should do too. Paul taught us to remember that every good thing we do isn't because of how great we are—but because God gives us the skill and talent to do it.

*Dear Jesus, please teach me to be humble and
to remember that it's because of Your help that
I'm able to accomplish good things. . .*

JESUS IS THE SAME AS GOD

Christ is as God is.
COLOSSIANS 1:15

It might be hard to imagine Jesus and God as one person. Paul wanted his friends to know that Jesus is part of and the same as God. When writing to his friends in a city called Colossae, Paul said Jesus was with God before anything was made. Like God, Jesus is a Spirit we can't see with our eyes. Paul said Jesus is the same as the God who created everything. He wrote, "Christ made everything in the heavens and on the earth. He made everything that is seen and things that are not seen. He made all the powers of heaven" (Colossians 1:16). Jesus is God Himself coming down to earth to be with us. Paul reminded his friends that Jesus is the only reason they would live in heaven someday.

Dear Jesus, I believe that You and God are one and the same. When I spend time with You, I'm spending time with God. . .

JESUS HAS PLANS FOR YOU

"'For I know the plans I have for you,' says the Lord, 'plans for well-being and not for trouble, to give you a future and a hope.'"
JEREMIAH 29:11

Jesus has plans for you and for everyone on earth. He won't let you know all at once what His plans are. But as you grow and learn, you will see His plans for your life unfold. He has already put inside you all the skill and talent you need. He knows everything about you from the day He created you until the day your body will die. Jesus knows what you will do when you grow up, if you will get married, who you will marry, how many children you will have. . . Sometimes, you will feel Jesus leading you in one direction or another. Listen for His voice inside your heart and follow where He leads.

Dear Jesus, I wonder what Your plans are for me. Help me follow wherever You lead. . .

JESUS, THE GOOD SHEPHERD

"I am the Lord your God, Who teaches you to do well, Who leads you in the way you should go."
ISAIAH 48:17

Long before Jesus came to earth, there was a king named David. He wrote psalms—songs to honor and worship the Lord. In one of his most famous psalms, David compared the Lord to a shepherd watching over his sheep. David reminded us that Jesus is like a good shepherd. A shepherd provides his sheep with everything they need: food, water, safety, comfort, goodness, kindness. . . A shepherd never leaves his sheep. He guides them along the right path. When Jesus lived on earth, He said to His disciples, "I am the Good Shepherd" (John 10:11, 14). Jesus watches over you all the time. He knows what you need. Jesus will always lead you in the right way. And if you should get lost, He knows where to find you.

Dear Jesus, I'm grateful that You are always with me and watching over me. . .

PSALM 23

The Lord is my Shepherd. I will
have everything I need.
PSALM 23:1

These are the words to Psalm 23 (SKJV), David's song about Jesus. Memorize them so you will always have them inside your heart:

The LORD is my shepherd. I shall not want. He makes me to lie down in green pastures. He leads me beside the still waters. He restores my soul. He leads me in the paths of righteousness for His name's sake. Yes, though I walk through the valley of the shadow of death, I will not fear evil, for You are with me. Your rod and Your staff, they comfort me. You prepare a table before me in the presence of my enemies. You anoint my head with oil. My cup runs over. Surely goodness and mercy shall follow me all the days of my life, and I will dwell in the house of the LORD forever.

Dear Jesus, whenever I feel lost or I need
Your help, I will remember Psalm 23. . .

DON'T GIVE UP

When we have learned not to give up,
it shows we have stood the test. When
we have stood the test, it gives us hope.
ROMANS 5:4

Paul spent the rest of his life working toward his goal—telling the world about Jesus. He never gave up. Paul taught his friends not to give up either. It's not always easy working toward a goal. Reaching a goal takes time, patience, and a lot of hard work. Getting through the hard places means testing yourself to see if you can get past any obstacles in your way. The more tests you pass, the stronger you will become. And with each goal you meet, you will gain hope that you can tackle another. If you ever feel like giving up, ask Jesus to help you keep going. With Him on your side, you can do anything!

Dear Jesus, if I feel like giving up, I will turn
to You for strength and hope. . .

PUT YOURSELF TO THE TEST

*Test everything and do not let good
things get away from you.*
1 THESSALONIANS 5:21

How much do you know about Jesus? As you've been reading this book, you've learned more about Him each day. On these next pages, try testing yourself to see how much you remember. Let's start at the beginning. See if you know the answer to this question: **What was Jesus' mother's name? Was it Elizabeth? Martha? Or Mary?** If you answered "Mary," you have the right answer! God's angel Gabriel came to Mary one day and said she had been chosen by God to give birth to His Son. She was to name the baby Jesus. Now, can you remember the town where Jesus was born? The correct answer is "Bethlehem." Jesus was born in Bethlehem in a stable or cave where animals were kept.

---

*Dear Jesus, I want to remember everything I've
learned about You. I want to share what I've
learned with my family and friends. . .*

SAVIOR OF THE WORLD

*"For we. . .know that this is indeed the
Christ, the Savior of the world."*
JOHN 4:42 SKJV

God sent Jesus to earth as a little baby with a big plan. On the night Jesus was born, angels told the shepherds who He was. The wise men who visited baby Jesus knew who He was too. Jesus was the Messiah, the Savior ancient prophets had written about in the Old Testament. God told the prophets long ago that He planned to send the Messiah to earth— someone He chose to save the world's people. Here is your question: **What did the world's people need to be saved from?** If you said "sin," you're correct! No one is perfect. Everyone sins—we all do things that go against God's rules. Instead of punishing us for breaking His rules, God sent Jesus, our Savior, to take the punishment we deserve.

---

*Dear Jesus, we call You our Savior because
You are the One who saves us from sin. . .*

FORGIVEN

*The person who keeps on sinning is
guilty of not obeying the Law of God.
For sin is breaking the Law of God.*

1 John 3:4

This next question is an easy one. **Can you name five things that are sins?** Remember, a sin is anything God isn't pleased to see or hear. Sadly, it's an easy question to answer because everyone is guilty of sinning. We can't stop ourselves from doing some of the things we know are wrong. There's not one person who has ever lived who has been perfect and not messed up and disappointed God. That's why we need Jesus. When we do or say things that displease God and we are sorry for our sins, we can ask Jesus to forgive us, and be sure that He will. Jesus promises us that whatever sin we are guilty of, we are already and forever forgiven if we believe in Him as our Savior.

Dear Jesus, there's no sin You won't forgive me for...

TEMPTATION

*"And do not lead us into temptation,
but deliver us from evil."*
MATTHEW 6:13 SKJV

Jesus went alone into the desert for forty days. While He was there, someone tempted Him to turn away from God. That someone questioned whether Jesus really is God's Son. He tried to get Jesus to prove it. But Jesus didn't have anything to prove! He said, "You must not tempt the Lord your God" (Matthew 4:7). Then that someone promised Jesus all the world's nations if Jesus would bow down and worship him. Jesus answered, "You must worship the Lord your God. You must obey Him only" (Matthew 4:10). **Who was that someone in the desert with Jesus?** Did you say "Satan" or "the devil"? Satan will always lead you toward sin. But Jesus gives you power to say, "Get away from me!" When you put your faith and trust in Jesus, He takes Satan's power away.

Dear Jesus, when Satan tempts me to sin, help me to not give in. Give me strength to say, "No!"...

TWELVE CHOSEN HELPERS

Jesus said to them, "Follow Me."
MATTHEW 4:19

Jesus chose twelve men to be His special helpers. We know these helpers by another name. **Can you fill in the missing word? Jesus' helpers were called His _____.** The correct answer is "disciples." But if you said "followers," that's okay too. It's a bonus if you can name some or all of them. They were Peter, Andrew, James (the son of Zebedee), John, Philip, Nathanael, Matthew, Thomas, James (the son of Alphaeus), Simon, Judas (the son of James), and Judas Iscariot. Jesus had planned all along who His disciples would be. Their role was to serve Jesus and to learn from Him so they could teach others. When you share what you know about Jesus and do your best to teach others to live in ways that are pleasing to God, then you are doing what Jesus' disciples did!

Dear Jesus, please lead me to serve You and to be a good example for others...

HAVE FAITH IN JESUS

[Jesus] said to them, "Where is your faith?"
LUKE 8:25

Jesus had been speaking to a crowd near a lake. He was tired and wanted to rest awhile. So, Jesus and His disciples got into their boat and set sail for the opposite shore. As they were sailing, Jesus fell asleep. While He slept, a windstorm came across the lake. The boat began filling with water, and the disciples were afraid. Here is your next question: **What did Jesus do after the disciples woke Him?** Your answer is correct if you said, "Jesus calmed the storm." He told the storm to stop, and it did. Then He asked His disciples, "Where is your faith?" They should have known they were safe while they were with Jesus. You are safe with Him too. Jesus is with you all the time. If you ever feel worried or afraid, call on Jesus. Ask Him to keep you calm.

Dear Jesus, I feel safe knowing You are with me. . .

THE GREATEST LAWS

*"All the Laws and the writings of
the early preachers depend on these
two most important Laws."*
MATTHEW 22:40

One day, the proud religious law-keepers asked Jesus, "Which is the greatest of God's laws?" Jesus answered that there were two, and everything else depends on them. He said the most important of God's laws is "You must love the Lord your God with all your heart and with all your soul and with all your mind" (Matthew 22:37). **Do you remember the second-greatest law? Fill in the blank with the correct word: "You must love your _____ as you love yourself."** Did you say "neighbor"? When God pours His love into your heart, you will want to share His love with others. With God's love inside your heart, it becomes easier to love your neighbor with God's kind of love—a love that is patient, forgiving, and kind.

---

*Dear Jesus, help me love my neighbor, and
everyone else, with Your kind of love. . .*

MIRACLE WORKER

*And my God will give you everything you need
because of His great riches in Christ Jesus.*
PHILIPPIANS 4:19

When Jesus was on earth, He performed miracles. Do you remember the story where He fed a crowd of five thousand? Jesus took a boy's lunch of five small loaves of bread and two fish, and He multiplied it again and again until everyone was fed. That's just one of many miracles Jesus did. Here is your next question: **Can you list three more miracles Jesus performed?** You probably thought of more than three. Jesus healed people. He cast out evil spirits. He even raised people from being dead. When His disciples went fishing and caught nothing, Jesus told them to cast their nets again. They caught so many fish their weight almost sunk the boat. Today, Jesus still does miracles. He knows exactly what you need, and He will provide it. Nothing is impossible for Him.

Dear Jesus, I trust You to provide everything I need...

MARTHA, MARTHA!

*Keep your minds thinking about things in
heaven. Do not think about things on the earth.*
COLOSSIANS 3:2

Jesus loved His friends Mary and Martha and their brother
Lazarus. When Jesus was in town, He visited them and
stayed at their house. You've heard the story: Jesus came
for dinner. Martha was busy making supper, while Mary
sat on the floor near Jesus listening to everything He said.
This irritated Martha. She wanted help with supper! So,
Martha asked Jesus to agree with her that Mary needed to
stop talking with Him and come help with supper. Jesus
answered: "Martha, Martha. . . . Only a few things are
important, even just one. Mary has chosen the good thing"
(Luke 10:41–42). Here is your question: **What was that
one good and important thing Mary had chosen?** Did
you answer "Jesus"? Spending time with Jesus and putting
Him first is more important than anything else.

*Dear Jesus, I will try my best to make You more
important than anything else in my life. . .*

THEY TURNED AGAINST HIM

"The world cannot hate you but it hates Me. I speak against the world because of its sinful works."

JOHN 7:7

Crowds came to hear Jesus speak. He talked about sin, pleasing God, and living right. Jesus did amazing miracles that no one else could do. He was popular and loved by many. But there was a small group who hated Him. This next question has multiple answers: **Why did they hate Jesus?** The proud religious law-keepers hated Him because He was becoming more popular than they were. They feared Jesus had more power over the people than they did. Some were jealous. Others felt they obeyed God's laws better than Jesus did. They thought Jesus was a liar instead of God's Son. Jesus had done nothing wrong, yet in the end the haters convinced others to turn against Him.

Dear Jesus, I won't turn against You. You didn't lie about who You are! You are God's Son, and Your love saved us from sin. . .

PALM SUNDAY

Be full of joy, O people... ! Call out in a loud voice... ! See, your King is coming to you. He is fair and good and has the power to save.

ZECHARIAH 9:9

Every year, Christians celebrate Palm Sunday. They remember Jesus riding into a famous city, where people laid palm branches down as a path to welcome Him. They honored Jesus as if He was their King. This question has two parts: **What city did Jesus go to? What was He riding on when He entered the city gates?** If you answered "Jerusalem" and "a donkey," you got both parts right. Jesus rode into Jerusalem on a donkey. The people called out, "Greatest One! The Son of David! Great and honored is He Who comes in the name of the Lord!" (Matthew 21:9). This worried the proud religious law-keepers, and they hated Jesus even more.

Dear Jesus, on Palm Sunday and every day, I welcome You into my heart. You are my Lord, Savior, and King...

TRAITOR!

They sat at the table and ate. Jesus said,
"For sure, I tell you, one of you will hand
Me over to be killed. He is eating with Me."
MARK 14:18

In Jerusalem, Jesus shared one last supper with His disciples. One of them was a traitor, a follower who pretended to be loyal to Jesus but was not. **What was his name?** Did you say "Judas Iscariot"? Judas made a deal with the proud religious law-keepers to lead soldiers to Jesus so they could arrest Him. They charged Jesus with lying about being the Savior God promised the world. They accused Him of wanting to destroy their temple and made up other lies about Him. None of it was a surprise to Jesus. He knew it would happen. But the other disciples were shocked and afraid when Jesus was arrested and taken away.

Dear Jesus, You are God, and You do not lie.
Everything You said to the law-keepers was true.
Every word You speak is perfect and true. . .

GOOD FRIDAY

"For see, darkness will cover the earth.
Much darkness will cover the people.
But the Lord will rise upon you, and His
shining-greatness will be seen upon you."
Isaiah 60:2

There are two questions left. The answers to both you will want to hold inside your heart forever. Ready for the first question? Each year on the Friday before Easter, Christians remember one of the most important events in Jesus' life. That Friday is called Good Friday. **What happened on that day?** Good Friday marks the day Jesus died on the cross. God allowed all the sin there ever was and ever will be to be poured into Jesus' heart, and He took the punishment for it that we deserve. Jesus did this because He loves us and wants us to be with Him forever in heaven someday.

Dear Jesus, Good Friday is a sad day because You suffered so much and died, but it's wonderful, too, because it's the day You saved us from sin. . .

EASTER

*"He who puts his trust in the Son
has life that lasts forever."*

JOHN 3:36

Here is your final question: **Why do we celebrate Easter Sunday?** There are many symbols people think of as part of the holiday. But the true meaning of Easter has nothing to do with candy, colored eggs, baskets, and bunnies. Easter is 100 percent all about Jesus. It marks the day Jesus came alive again, just as He'd said He would. On Resurrection Sunday, people saw and talked with Jesus. Every word ever spoken about God's promised Messiah came true that day. He was certainly, truly God's Son, our Savior. And when Jesus went back up to heaven, it was a reminder to His followers that after they die, they will go up to heaven, too, to live with Jesus forever. Easter is the most joyful of all days because it represents His promise of eternal (forever) life.

Dear Jesus, thank You for reminding me that Easter is all about You and Your gift of life forever in heaven. . .

FOREVER

"I give them life that lasts forever. They will never be punished. No one is able to take them out of My hand."

JOHN 10:28

Jesus' gift of forever life in heaven is—forever. You will never again have a body that gets old, hurt, or sick. In heaven you will have a new body that cannot die. Just like everything else in heaven, it will be perfect. When you believe in Jesus as the one who came to save you from sin, Jesus' gift of forever life can't be taken from you. It is yours to keep. Even if you mess up and displease Him again and again, Jesus won't take back His gift of forever. Jesus has already taken the punishment you deserve for every sin you will ever commit. You don't have to worry that He won't welcome you into heaven. When Jesus comes into your heart, you are His forever.

---

*Dear Jesus, it's hard to imagine forever.
I wonder what it's like...*

HEAVEN

*"By His breath the heavens
are made beautiful."*
JOB 26:13

Nothing on earth can compare with the perfect beauty of heaven. The Bible tells us only a little of what heaven is like. All the homes there are big and beautiful. Jesus already has a house picked out and ready for you when you get there. Heaven is a city with pearl gates and golden streets. God rules heaven, and all its citizens worship Him. Heaven is a place of peace and joy where people get along. There is no evil in heaven, only good. Nothing will get in the way of us communicating in heaven. We will all speak the same language. In heaven, we will forever be with those who love Jesus and believe in His promise of forever life. Much of heaven we can only imagine. What do you think it looks like?

Dear Jesus, I wonder, what does my house in heaven look like? What special and wonderful things are waiting for me there? . . .

JESUS IS COMING BACK

So be on your guard! You don't know
when your Lord will come.
MATTHEW 24:42 CEV

Jesus is coming back to earth someday, not just as Spirit but with a body people can see. Everyone will know when He comes. He is coming down from heaven with an army of angels riding white horses and dressed in fine, white linen. Jesus is coming back to be the judge of everything evil. He will reign over all nations as their mighty and perfect King. Even then, some people on earth will not believe or have faith in Jesus. In the end, Jesus will destroy Satan and all those who have no faith. He will create a new heaven and a new earth where all believers will live forever. When will it happen? The Bible doesn't tell us. But those who love Jesus and put their faith in Him will be ready.

Dear Jesus, I want everyone to have faith in You so they will have a place in heaven someday. . .

JESUS LOVES YOU

*"The one who loves Me is the one who
has My teaching and obeys it. My Father
will love whoever loves Me. I will love
him and will show Myself to him."*

JOHN 14:21

Jesus was there when you were created. He has been with you every day of your life, and He will be with you forever. Jesus loves you with a special kind of love no one else has. His love for you is perfect. When you ask Him to come into your heart, His love will fill it to overflowing. Jesus' love will help you become more loving toward others too. You will never have to worry that Jesus loves others more than He loves you, because He has the amazing ability to give all His love to each of His children all at the same time. Jesus loves you! Believe it!

---

*Dear Jesus, Your love is like no other love. It fills
my heart with joy. Jesus, I love You too. . .*

KEEP LEARNING

*Have I not written to you great things
of wise teaching and much learning?*
PROVERBS 22:20

You've learned so much about Jesus by spending just three minutes a day with Him. Don't stop now! Keep learning. Jesus has a lifetime of learning waiting for you if you'll stay near to Him, follow where He leads you, and obey His words. The Bible is one way Jesus communicates with you. When you read its words and think about them, Jesus will use the Bible to guide you. Read the first four books of the New Testament. These are known as the Gospels. They tell about Jesus' life and the good news that He saved us from sin. Talk with Jesus not just once a day but all day. He hears you even when you pray silently in your thoughts. Remember—Jesus is your best friend today and forever. He will never leave you or let you down.

---

*Dear Jesus, our friendship is just
beginning. Let's make it grow. . .*

SHARE THE GOOD NEWS!

*Let the message about Christ completely
fill your lives, while you use all your
wisdom to teach and instruct each other.*
COLOSSIANS 3:16 CEV

Jesus came to save everyone from the punishment of sin. He spent His time on earth teaching the right way to live. Jesus knew humans aren't perfect. Everyone messes up. That's why He took all the world's sin into His heart and allowed it to die along with Him on the cross. Jesus did that so all who believe in Him will never be punished by God for their sins. Jesus' death on the cross means those who believe are already forgiven and have a forever place in heaven. Jesus wants everyone to know about Him and what He did. So, share with your friends and family what you've learned! They might want to know Jesus and have a forever home in heaven too.

Dear Jesus, I'm ready to share the good news. Let's go!...

SCRIPTURE INDEX

OLD TESTAMENT

DEUTERONOMY
31:8..143

JOSHUA
24:15..120

1 KINGS
19:11–12..154

JOB
13:17..90
26:13..184

PSALMS
2:7..24
23:1..167
33:12..56
34:18..59
37:5..51
41:9..118
56:3..40
78:1–2..88
139:4..35

PROVERBS
3:5–6..39
22:11..63
22:20..187
24:21..100

ISAIAH
29:12..137

ISAIAH
7:14..8
9:2..29
9:6..12
30:9..106
41:10..45
48:17..166
52:7..102
53:3..124
53:12..126
55:7..113
60:2..181

JEREMIAH
29:11..165

HOSEA
11:1..17

AMOS
3:7..31

MICAH
5:2..9

ZECHARIAH
9:9......................................103, 179

NEW TESTAMENT

MATTHEW
2:2..15
2:23..18
4:19..173
5:3..58, 163

5:5..60
5:6..61
5:7..62
5:10..65
5:13–14..67

5:33	69
5:39	70
5:44	66
6:1	71
6:5	72
6:8	162
6:12	159
6:13	172
6:21	73
6:33	91
6:34	74
7:1	75
7:12	76
7:29	89
9:13	48
9:28	158
11:28	84
11:29	43
14:31	96
16:6	54
16:21	132
22:40	175
23:13	107
24:42	185
26:41	28
26:56	129
26:75	121
27:66	133

MARK

1:27	44
1:34	85
3:6	86
4:40	95
14:18	180
14:61–62	122
15:2	123
15:34	127
16:15	142
16:16	23

LUKE

1:17	20

1:65–66	21
2:6–7	10
2:11	11
2:32	13
2:38	14
4:8	16
4:24	41
5:24	53
7:16	83
8:25	174
9:20	79
9:35	81
9:60	97
17:5	80
19:10	92
22:19	110
22:28	111
23:34	125
23:46	128
24:25	136
24:34	140

JOHN

1:15	25
1:23	22
2:11	32
3:3	36
3:16	7
3:36	182
4:14	38
4:42	170
5:18	114
5:23	55
6:14	78
6:38	19
6:64	101
7:7	178
7:16	57
8:12	104
8:31	30
8:44	26
10:28	183
11:25	99

12:44	105
13:7	34
13:13	109
13:34–35	160
14:1	116
14:21	186
15:21	119
16:8	115
16:33	157
17:1	117
20:29	141

Acts

1:4	145
2:18	147
2:33	146
2:37	148
2:47	149
3:26	150
9:4	152
9:15	153
13:29	131

Romans

5:4	168
5:8	49
6:6	108
6:9	134
6:10–11	135
10:9	138
11:29	46
13:10	93

1 Corinthians

3:17	33
11:1	155
13:4–8	112

2 Corinthians

5:7	82

Galatians

2:20	144
3:26	64

Ephesians

2:8	94
4:26	68
6:18	161

Philippians

1:12	156
4:6	98
4:19	77, 176

Colossians

1:15	164
3:2	177
3:16	188

1 Thessalonians

5:21	169

1 Timothy

1:17	139

Hebrews

4:15	27
13:5	42
13:8	52

James

1:6	50, 87
1:17	47

1 Peter

4:16	130

2 Peter

1:21	151

1 John

3:1	37
3:4	171

ABOUT THE AUTHOR

Jean Fischer has a long career in the publishing industry, first as an editor and creative manager and currently as a freelance writer and consultant for leading Christian publishers. She has written many devotional books for children and adults and has cowritten books with Sarah Young, Sheila Walsh, and others. When she isn't writing, Jean enjoys gardening and visiting the lakes and forests in northern Wisconsin.